Amazon Reviews for The Supernatural

...Wonderful!!

...Another masterpiece from my favourite author!

...Absolutely enthralling, brilliant read!

...Superb content based on Anglo-Saxon lore

...A incredible source of Anglo-Saxon traditions and folklore compiled in a simple to read book.

...Gods, faeries, people and events are some the topics included. Those shed a light on how the Anglo-Saxon world was.

...Great chapters involving some of the world's most infamous traditions such as Halloween and Christmas.

...A great read that might need an index because of the vast amount of the subjects covered.

Front cover image by author and illustrator,
Carl Emil Doepler, 1824-1905

Copyright © 2017 by S. A. Swaffington
All rights reserved. This book or any portion thereof may not be reproduced or used in any manner whatsoever without the express written permission of the author, except for the use of brief quotations in a book review or for use on social media.

ISBN: 9781973588467

The Supernatural World of the Anglo-Saxons

Gods, Folklore and the Pagan Roots of Christmas and Halloween

S. A. Swaffington

…urum þeóde…
…for our people…

Introduction
Who Were the Anglo-Saxons?

The term 'Anglo-Saxon' is a modern term used to describe the Germanic settlers of Britain, from the mid-5th Century, to their creation of the modern English Nation, to the Norman Conquest of 1066. These Germanic clans, including the Jutes, Angles, Saxons, Frīsians, Franks and others, came to Britain from what is now Denmark, North Germany and the Netherlands. The Anglo-Saxons referred to themselves in their writings as 'Angelcynn', meaning 'English kin'. It was the Angles who gave their name to the Anglo-Saxon Kingdom of East Anglia and to the Kingdom of Ængla land - England.

'From the Saxon land, the district now known as Old Saxony, came the East Saxons (Essex), the South Saxons (Sussex) and the West Saxons (Wessex). Besides this, from the Land of the Angles, the land between the Kingdoms of the Jutes and the Saxons (Denmark), which is called Angeln, came the East Angles, the Middle Angles, the Mercians, and all the Northumbrian race, as well as the other Anglian tribes. Angeln is said to have remained deserted from that day to this. Their first leaders are said to have been two brothers, Hengist and Horsa. Horsa was afterwards killed in battle by the Britons. In the eastern part of Kent there is still a monument bearing his name. They were the sons of Wihtgils, of Witta, of Wecta, of Wōden, from whose stock the royal families of many kingdoms claimed their descent.' - The Venerable Bede, 673-735, the first English historian, The Ecclesiastical History of the English People

The Anglo-Saxons had been Pagans on Continental Europe for centuries and brought their Gods, beliefs, stories and culture with them to Britain before converting to Christianity. The most famous stories are, of course, Bēowulf, Ket and Wīg, and the story of Offa the First, all of which are set on the European Continent.

'Sometimes at pagan shrines they vowed offerings to idols, swore oaths that the killer of souls might come to their aid and save the people. That was their way.' - Bēowulf, a heroic poem composed in England by Christian monks, between the 7th and 10th Century A. D.

The first mention of the English people was first written by the Roman historian, Cornelius Tacitus, who wrote about the Germanic Clans that existed in the 1st Century.

'The Langabardi (Long-beards) are distinguished by the fewness of their numbers. Ringed round as they are by many mighty clans, they find safety, not in submission, but in battle and its perils. After them come the Reudigni (Rondings), Auiones (Eowan), Angli (Angles/English), Varni (Wærne), Eudoses (Jutes), Suarines, and Nuithones (Teutons), well-guarded by rivers and forests. There is nothing remarkable about these clans, unless it is the common worship of Nerthuz or Earth Mother.'

It is recorded in The Anglo-Saxon Chronicle that the Anglo-Saxons began to settle Britain in the year 449, led by the brothers Hengist and Horsa and continued to settle for over two hundred years. But archaeological evidence suggests that Saxons had settled Britain at Wēste Stōw, in what is now West Suffolk, England, around 420 A. D., only ten years after the Romans abandoned Britain to its fate. 'Wēste Stōw' is Old English for 'deserted place', which makes sense as we know many young men left Britain in order to fight in Europe after the decline of the Western Roman Empire.

'The Almighty Judge of good deeds and bad, the Lord God, Head of the Heavens and High King of the world, was unknown to them.' - The Anglo-Saxon poem, Bēowulf

In the late 6th Century, Pope Gregory encountered a group of young English boys that were about to be sold as slaves in Rome. Impressed by their fair skin, blonde hair and blue eyes, the Pope asked where they came from. Hearing they were Angles from Ængla land, the Pope said in Latin, 'Non Anglii, sed angeli', which translates, 'Not Angles, but Angels.' That year, the Pope sent Saint Augustine and a large group of missionaries to the Kingdom of Kent, to convert the English to Christianity. In the year 597, Hengist's great-grandson, King Æthelbert of Kent, met Saint Augustine and his monks in open air so the wind could blow away any spells from their foreign magic. King Æthelbert later replied to Saint Augustine with a letter:

'The words and promises you bring are fair enough, but because they are new to us and doubtful, I cannot consent to accept them and forsake those beliefs which I and the whole English race have held so long.'

A letter from Pope Gregory to Mellitus reads:

'The idol temples of that race (the English) should by no means be destroyed, but only the idols in them. Take holy water and sprinkle it in these shrines, build altars and place relics in them. For if the shrines are well built, it is essential that they should be changed from the worship of devils to the service of the true God. When the people see that their shrines are not destroyed they will be able to banish error from their hearts and be more ready to come to the places they are familiar with, but now recognizing and worshipping the true God.'

In the year 627, King Edwin asked Cofi, the chief priest at the great Temple of Wōden at Goodmanham, Northumbria, if he should convert to Christianity or not. Cofi told the King that he should instantly give up the old religion and he (Cofi) volunteered to fire the Pagan temple and altars himself.

'Then in contempt of his vain superstitions, he (Cofi) desired the King to furnish him with arms and a stallion, that he might mount and go forth to destroy the idols; for it was not lawful before for the high priest to carry arms, or to ride on anything but a mare. Having, therefore, girt a sword about him, with a spear in his hand, he mounted the King's stallion and went his way to the idols. The multitude, beholding it, thought he was mad; but as soon as he drew near the temple, he didn't delay to desecrate it by casting into it the spear which he held; and rejoicing in the knowledge of the worship of the true God, he commanded his companions to tear down and set on fire the temple, with all its precincts. This place where the idols once stood is still shown, not far from York, to the east, beyond the river Derwent, and is now called Godmunddingaham, where the high priest, by the inspiration of the true God, profaned and destroyed the altars which he had himself consecrated.' - The Venerable Bede, Ecclesiastical History of the English People

Less than a century later, the whole of England was officially Christian. As the Western Roman Empire slowly collapsed across Europe, a new Empire rose in its place, a Christian Empire, one still based in Rome. Turning the continent Christian was a bloody and violent process; however, in England the process was, for the most part, peaceful. It seems the English offered little, if any, resistance. Once Christianity became the dominant religion, Christians did not tolerate any competition. A list of 'Punishments for heathens and others who turn from the Church of God', 690, states:

'If anyone, in ignorance, eats or drinks by a heathen shrine, they are to promise never to do so again and to do forty days penance on bread and water. If it is deliberately done again, that is, after a priest has declared that it is a sacrilege and the place of demons, the offender shall do penance on bread and water for thrice forty days. But if it is done to glorify the idol, the penance shall be for three years.'

In the early 8th Century, the Anglo-Saxon missionary, Saint Boniface, from Devon, England, along with his followers, travelled to what is now Germany in order to convert the Germanic Pagans to Christianity. In 724, Saint Boniface cut down their sacred tree, known as Thunor's Oak, located in what is now Hesse, Germany. Thunor comes for the Old English 'Þunor', the equivalent of the Norse 'Thor', God of thunder and lightning. Wood from the oak was then used to build a Christian church at the site and was dedicated to Saint Peter. The 8th Century Vita Bonifatii auctore Willibaldi reads:

'Now at that time many of the Hessians, brought under the Catholic faith and confirmed by the grace of the sevenfold spirit, received the laying on of hands; others indeed, not yet strengthened in soul, refused to accept in their entirety the lessons of the inviolate faith. Moreover some were wont secretly, some openly to sacrifice to trees and springs; some in secret, others openly practised inspections of victims and divinations, legerdemain and incantations; some turned their attention to auguries and auspices and various sacrificial rites; while others, with sounder minds, abandoned all the profanations of heathenism, and committed none of these things. With the advice and counsel of these last, the saint attempted, in the place called Gaesmere, while the servants of God stood by his side, to fell a certain oak of extraordinary size, which is called, by an old name of the Pagans, the Oak of Jupiter (Thunor). And when in the strength of his steadfast heart he had cut the lower notch, there was present a great multitude of Pagans, who in their souls were earnestly cursing the enemy of their gods. But when the fore-side of the tree was notched only a little, suddenly the oak's vast bulk, driven by a blast from above, crashed to the ground, shivering its crown of branches as it fell; and, as if by the gracious compensation of the Most High, it burst into four parts, and four trunks of huge size, equal in length, were seen, unwrought by the brethren who stood by. At this sight the Pagans who before had cursed now, on the contrary, believed, and blessed the Lord, and put away their former reviling. Then moreover the most holy bishop, after taking counsel with the brethren, built from the timber of the tree wooden oratory, and dedicated it in honour of Saint Peter the apostle.'

In the year 772, during his thirty year campaign to force the Saxons into accepting Christianity, the Frankish King, Charlemagne (Charles the Great), destroyed the Saxon holy pillar, known as Irminsul, a sacred tree trunk in Saxon Paganism. Ten years after the destruction of Irminsul, and fifty years after the arrival of Saint Boniface to convert the Saxons, King Charlemagne defeated the rebellious Saxons. Charlemagne ordered them to convert to Christianity or be beheaded. It is recorded in the Royal Frankish Annals the death of four thousand, five hundred Saxons. The slaughter and genocide took place on October 782, in what is now Lower Saxony, Germany, by the river Aller, in Verden. It is known today as The Massacre of Verden.

'When he heard this, the Lord King Charles rushed to the place with all the Franks that he could gather on short notice and advanced to where the Aller flows into the Weser. Then all the Saxons came together again, submitted to the authority of the Lord King, and surrendered the evildoers who were chiefly responsible for this revolt to be put to death - four thousand and five hundred of them. This sentence was carried out. Widukind was not among them, since he had fled to Nordmannia (Denmark). When he had finished this business, the Lord King returned to Francia.' - The Royal Frankish Annals
8th and 9th Century

Several years later, a Royal chronicler commenting on Charlemagne's treatment of the Saxons, states:

'...either they were defeated or subjected to the Christian religion or completely swept away.'

King Charlemagne is known today as the 'Slaughterer of the Saxons'. As stated above, the great Saxon warrior, and leader of the resistance, Widukind, fled to Denmark, no doubt telling tales of the terrible, unspeakable things that had been happening to his people for the last thirty years. Interestingly, only five years after the Massacre of Verden, the first Viking vessel lands on the coast of Christian England.

'787 A. D. This year King Bertric (Beorhtric, King of Wessex, 786-802) took Edburga, the daughter of Offa, to wife. And in his days came first three ships of the Northmen from the land of robbers. The reve (shire reve/sheriff) then rode thereto, and would drive them to the King's town; for he knew not what they were; and there he was slain. These were the first ships of the Danish men that sought the land of the English Nation.' - The Anglo-Saxon Chronicle

Six years later, the Holy Island of Lindisfarne, on the east coast of England, in the Kingdom of Northumbria, was raided by Vikings, led by Ragnar Lothbrok, resulting in the slaughter of the Christian monks who worshipped there.

'793 A. D. This year came dreadful fore-warnings over the land of the Northumbrians, terrifying the people most woefully: these were immense sheets of light rushing through the air, and whirlwinds, and fiery dragons flying across the firmament. These tremendous tokens were soon followed by a great famine: and not long after, on the sixth day before the ides of January in the same year, the harrowing inroads of heathen men made lamentable havoc in the church of God in Holy-island, by rapine and slaughter.' - The Anglo Saxon Chronicle

The Viking Age had begun and no place in Europe was safe from the Fury of the Northmen, including the Kingdom of the Franks, which was raided numerous times. But no place was more affected than England. For centuries, the Vikings terrorized, looted, raped and pillaged the English people, giving rise to great heroes, such as Earl Byrhtnoth and Ælfred the Great, amongst many others, who stood against the Vikings.

In 886, England was split into two halves, one English, the other subject to Danelaw and ruled by several Viking chieftains. The Danelaw was based on the treaty between Ælfred the Great and the Danish warlord, Guthrum, following Guthrum's defeat at the Battle of Edington in 878. In 886, the Treaty of Ælfred and Guthrum was formalised, defining the boundaries of their Kingdoms, with the intension of creating peace between the two halves. The Danelaw comprised of fourteen shires - York, Nottingham, Derby, Lincoln, Essex, Cambridge, Suffolk, Norfolk, Northampton, Huntingdon, Bedford, Hertford, Middlesex and Buckingham. Many place-names under the Danelaw are of Norse origin, such as places ending with 'ness', 'thorpe', 'holme', 'toft' and 'thwaite'. Hundreds of new words now entered the English language, such as 'husband', 'sky', 'gate', 'skull', 'muck', and many others.

In the year 937, Ælfred the Great's grandsons, King Æthelstān and Ēadmund, led the Anglo-Saxons to victory over the combined armies of the Welsh, Scots, Irish and Vikings, forcing Constantine II, King of Scots, to surrender at the Battle of Brunanburh, finally achieving their grandfather's vision by uniting the Anglo-Saxon Kingdoms as one nation, England, the world's first nation state.

By 1066, shortly after a great English victory against the Viking leader, Harold Hardrada, at the Battle of Stamford Bridge, William the Duke of Normandy, with the Pope's blessing, invaded England on the south coast. After battling with the Vikings and travelling for three days, the exhausted English army were defeated at the Battle of Hastings by William the Conqueror. William was crowned the new King of England on Christmas Day. After the Norman Invasion, the English were stripped of their land and were forced to make up the Working Class (peasantry) of England. To this day, 70% of land owned in England belongs to the Normans' descendants.

During the Winter of 1069/70, King William ordered the Harrying of the North, described by many scholars as an act of genocide against the English people. Writing about the Harrying of the North, over fifty years later, the Anglo-Norman chronicler, Orderic Vitalis, 1075-1142, said:

'The King stopped at nothing to hunt his enemies. He cut down many people and destroyed homes and land. Nowhere else had he shown such cruelty. This made a real change. To his shame, William made no effort to control his fury, punishing the innocent with the guilty. He ordered that crops and herds, tools and food be burned to ashes. More than 100,000 people perished of starvation. I have often praised William in this book, but I can say nothing good about this brutal slaughter. God will punish him.'

William's deathbed confession:

'I have persecuted the natives of England beyond all reason, whether gentle or simple. I have cruelly oppressed them and unjustly disinherited them, killed innumerable multitudes by famine or the sword and become the barbarous murderer of many thousands, both young and old of that fine race of people.'

The English people have been victims of Britain's ruling elite since the Norman Conquest in 1066 and, due to the conversion to Christianity, the indigenous faith of the English people has been victim of persecution and ridicule for even longer. As a result, the English have lost much of our faith and culture. Whatever crimes have been committed by Britain's ruling elite, including those against Scotland, Wales and Ireland, has been blamed on the English people ever since. The purpose of this book is to shed light on the Anglo-Saxons' beliefs before and after the conversion to Christianity. The English people come from a rich cultural tradition that we are only just starting to remember. And remember we must.

Part One
The Old Gods and Goddesses of England

Wōden

Wōden was the Chief God of the Anglo-Saxons and was associated with rage, fury and war, human sacrifice, hanging and death, but also healing and magic, royalty, knowledge and wisdom, poetry and the runic alphabet. Wōden is depicted carrying a long wooden staff and wearing a long grey coat, with a large grey hat or hood, and has one eye missing. Norse literature describes him sacrificing one eye to the Well of Wisdom in order to attain knowledge, which he then uses to create middle-Earth, the realm of mankind. He is also often depicted wearing an ancient Germanic eagle-feathered headdress, such as the one on the front cover of this book.

The name Wōden comes from the Old English 'wōd' meaning 'rage', 'mad' or 'furious'. There can be no doubt, the English 'Wōden' and the Norse 'Odin', are one and the same. In Old Saxon he was known as Wōdan. In Old High German he was known as Wuotan or Wōtan, meaning 'to rage'. The Vandals knew him as Godan. Wōden also had many nicknames, such as The Rune Master, Grim and the All-Father, amongst many others. In Norse Mythology, Odin is also known as Grímnir. Today, when we say something is grim, we mean deathly, sinister, fierce, savage or cruel. This may come from the Old English 'grimme', a term found in the Bēowulf poem.

In the 12th Century Icelandic Saga, Heimskringla, written by the poet and historian, Snorri Sturluson, Wōden is credited with having established the burial rites:

'He decreed that all the dead should be burned and placed on the funeral pyre with all their possessions. He also said that everyone should come into Valhalla (the Hall of the Slain) with all the property that he had on the pyre, and he should also enjoy the use of what he himself had buried in the earth, and the ashes should be carried out to sea or buried in the earth, and mounds should be raised in memory of men of rank. And there should be a sacrifice at the beginning of winter for a successful year, and at Midwinter (Yule) for regeneration, and a third in summer which was a sacrifice for victory.'

Snorri's account matches the descriptions by Cornelius Tacitus writing in the 1st Century:

'There is no pomp or splendour about their funerals. The one rule observed is that the bodies of famous men are burned with special kinds of wood. When they have heaped up the fire, they don't throw robes or spices on the top; but only a man's weapons, and sometimes his horse, are cast into the flames. The tomb is a raised mound of turf. They disdain to show honour by laboriously rearing high monuments of stone, because they think stone lies heavy on the dead. Weeping and wailing are soon abandoned, sorrow and mourning linger. A woman may decently express her grief in public; a man should nurse his in his heart.'

It is likely that Germania was written in response to the Romans losing a great battle against the Germanic tribes in the year 9 A. D., known as the Battle of the Teutoburg Forest.

Arminius was the son of a Germanic chieftain, who led an alliance of Germanic tribes to a historical victory against three invading Roman legions, consisting of twenty thousand men. After the battle, the Germanic warriors stripped the invading Romans naked and either hung them from trees as a sacrifice to Wōden, or tossed them into wolf pits to be killed and eaten by wolves.

Though Arminius was ultimately unsuccessful in forging a long-term union with the Germanic tribes, he is remembered in Germany today as a national hero and is honoured in the Hall of Fame, Walhalla, in Bavaria. Arminius wasn't an English figure and predates the coming of the Saxons to Britain by over four centuries; however, he is a common ancestor that is shared between the people of Germany and England and should be remembered as such.

Both the wolf and the raven were sacred animals of Wōden. In Norse Mythology, Geri and Freki (Ravenous and Greedy-One) are two wolves who accompany Wōden, while the two ravens, Huginn and Muninn (Thought and Memory), bring news to him. There is a small reference to this in the Bēowulf poem:

'The harp won't waken warriors, but the raven winging darkly over the doomed will have news, tidings for the eagle of how he hoked and ate, how the wolf and he made short work of the dead.'

Ravens were often seen on battlefields and naturally became associated with wolves, death and the war God, Wōden. Seeing a raven or an owl became a bad omen, for it meant the Gods were taking notice of something that was about to happen. Wōden can be seen on the front cover of this book, sitting upon his throne, alongside his two ravens and two wolves.

The great Anglo-Saxon Kings, long after converting to Christianity, claimed to be direct descendants of Wōden, listing him as a divine ancestor in their genealogies, including the Kingdoms of Wessex, Kent, East Anglia and Mercia.

There can be no doubt that Wōden was worshipped in Anglo-Saxon England, as his name is still etched upon the English landscape. The following is a list of place-names associated with Wōden in England:

Wambrook, Somerset - Wōden's Brook
Wampool, Hampshire - Wōden's Pool
Wanborough, Wiltshire - Wōden's Barrow
Wansdyke - Wōden's Dyke, an embankment
Wanstead, Essex - Wōden's Stead
Wednesbury, West Midlands - Wōden's burgh/strong-hold
Wednesfield, Wolverhampton, West Midlands - Wōden's field
Wednesham, Cheshire - Wōden's Ham
Wensley, Derbyshire - Wōden's meadow
Wembury, Devon - Wōden's Hill/Barrow
Wōden Hill, Hampshire, is a hill in Bagshot Heath. A valley which the West Overton-Alton road runs through was called Wōdnes-denu - Wōden's Valley
Wonston, Hampshire - Wōden's Town
Woodbridge, Suffolk - Wōden's Bridge
Woodnesborough, Kent - Wōden's burgh/strong-hold. The centre of the town was known as Wōden's Hill
Woodway House, Devon, from the house on Wōden's Way
Wormshill, Kent - Wōden's hill
Wormhill, Derbyshire - Wōden's hill
Grimsdyke, London - Grim's Dyke/earthwork/ditch
Grimes Graves, Norfolk
Grimsbury, Oxfordshire - Grim's strong-hold
Grimsbury Castle, Berkshire. An Iron Age hill-fort named after Wōden by the Saxons
Grimsby, Lincolnshire - named during the Viking Age
Grimley, Worcestershire, from the Old English 'Grimanleage', meaning the 'clearing of Grim'
Grimspound, an Iron Age settlement on Dartmoor
Grimscote, Northamptonshire - Grim's Cott
Grimsthorpe, Lincolnshire - Grim's Village

The Nine Herbs Charm is an Old English charm recorded in the 10th Century Lacnunga Manuscript. The charm is intended for treating those with infections or who have been poisoned by a preparation of nine herbs. The poem contains references to Christian and English Pagan elements. According to R. K. Gordon, 'the poem is clearly an old heathen thing which has been subjected to Christian censorship.'

The Nine Herbs Charm
translated from Old English

'Remember, Mugwort, what you made known,
what you arranged at the Great proclamation.
You were called Una, the oldest of herbs,
you have power against three and against thirty,
you have power against poison and against infection,
you have power against the loathsome foe roving through the land.

And you, Plantain, mother of herbs,
open from the east, mighty inside.
Over you chariots creaked, over you queens rode,
over you brides cried out, over you bulls snorted.
You withstood all of them, you dashed against them.
May you likewise withstand poison and infection
and the loathsome foe roving through the land.

Stune is the name of this herb, it grew on a stone,
it stands up against poison, it dashes against poison.
Nettle it is called, it attacks against poison,
it drives out the hostile one, it casts out poison.
This is the herb that fought against the serpent,
it has power against poison, it has power against infection,
it has power against the loathsome foe roving through the land.
Put to flight now, Venom-loather, the greater poisons,
though you are the lesser, until he is cured of both.

Remember, Chamomile, what you made known,
what you accomplished at Alorford,
that never a man should lose his life from infection
after Chamomile was prepared for his food.
This is the herb that is called Wergulu.
A seal sent it across the sea-right,
a vexation to poison, a help to others.
It stands against pain, it dashes against poison.

A worm came crawling, it killed nothing.
For Wōden took nine glory-twigs,
he smote the adder that it flew apart into nine parts.
There the Apple accomplished it against poison
that she, the loathsome serpent, would never dwell in the house.

Chervil and Fennel, two of much might,
they were created by the wise Lord,
holy in heaven as He hung;
He set and sent them to the seven worlds,
to the wretched and the fortunate, as a help to all.
It stands against pain, it fights against poison,
it avails against three and against thirty,
against foe's hand and against noble scheming,
against enchantment of vile creatures.

Now nine herbs have power against nine evil spirits,
against nine poisons and against nine infections:
against the red poison, against the foul poison,
against the white poison, against the pale blue poison,
against the yellow poison, against the green poison,
against the black poison, against the blue poison,
against the brown poison, against the crimson poison,
against worm-blister, against water-blister,
against thorn-blister, against thistle-blister,
against ice-blister, against poison-blister.

If any poison comes flying from the east,
or any from the north, or any from the south,
or any from the west among the people.
Christ stood over diseases of every kind.

I alone know a running stream,
and the nine adders beware of it.
May all the weeds spring up from their roots,
the seas slip apart, all saltwater,
when I blow this poison from you.

Mugwort, plantain open from the east, lamb's cress, venom-loather, camomile, nettle, crab-apple, chevil and fennel, old soap; pound the herbs to a powder, mix them with the soap and the juice of an apple. Then prepare a paste of water and ashes, take fennel, boil it with the paste and wash it with a beaten egg when you apply the salve, both before and after. Sing this charm three times on each of the herbs before you prepare them, and likewise on the apple. And sing the same charm into the mouth of the man and into both of his ears, and on the wound, before you apply the salve.'

In the Old Norse poem, Hávamál (Utterings of the High One), Odin offers advice for living, proper conduct and wisdom. Verses 138 and 139 reads:

'I know that I hung on a wind-gnarled tree nine long nights, wounded with a spear, dedicated to Odin, myself to myself, on that tree of which no man knows from where its roots run.

No bread did they give me, nor a drink from a horn, downwards I peered; I took up the runes, screaming I took them.'

The figure we know today as Santa Claus or Father Christmas riding the dark night sky with his eight reindeer is based on Wōden and his eight-legged steed, Slippery-One. During Yule, what we now call Christmas, Wōden could be seen leading the Wild Hunt and a procession of the dead across the Winter sky, in mad pursuit of trolls and fairies. In the Nordic countries, children used to fill old boots with hay for Odin's horse. In exchange for the hay, Odin would leave a small gift as a thank you.

Interestingly, in the Netherlands, Odin became known as Sinterklaas and rode a horse. The horse is still remembered to this day in popular culture.

'We're dashing through the snow in a one-horse open sleigh and over the fields we go, laughing all the way.'

Jingle Bells
(originally known as 'One Horse Open Sleigh')
by James Lord Pierpont, 1822-1893

Sinterklaas also carries a staff and has mischievous helpers with black faces, who listen down chimneys to find out whether children are bad or good and report to him, much like Odin's ravens who reported to the All-Father. In the 1950s, French priests claimed that Santa wasn't a Christian figure and so must be a creature of the Devil. They built a bonfire and burned a Santa figure on it.

English author and Anglo-Saxon professor, J. R. R. Tolkien, author of Lord of the Rings and The Hobbit, based his wizard character, Gandalf, on Wōden, the Lord of Magic.

It is important to remember that Wōden was a God of war, but he was also married to Frīge, the Goddess of peace. Wōden is remembered in England today as the God who gave his name to the English day of the week, Wednesday, from the Old English 'Wōdnesdæg', meaning 'Wōden's Day'.

Thunor

Thor, the Norse God of thunder and lightning, from the Old Norse, Þórr, was worshipped by the English under the name ðunor or Thunor. He was known in Old High German as Donar, in Old Saxon as Thunar, and Old Frīsian as Thuner, all of which come from the Proto-Germanic root word for thunder - þunraz (thunraz).

Not much of Thunor's cult survives in England, but he did give his name to the English day of the week, Thursday, from the Old English 'Thunoresdæg', meaning 'Thunor's Day'. In English place-names, Thunor gave his name to Thundersley in Essex, from the Old English 'Thunores Hlæw', meaning 'Thunor's Pillar' or 'Thunor's Sacred Tree'.

The Canterbury Charm is an Old English charm that was found inserted in the margin of an Anglo-Saxon manuscript from the year 1073, in Canterbury, Kent, England. It is clear that the author believed Thor to be a great magical healer:

>'Cyril wound-cause, go now!
>You are found.
>May Thor bless you, lord of ogres!
>Gyril wound-causer.
>Against blood-vessel pus!'

In Gilton, Kent, small amulets which resemble Thunor's hammer have been found in an Anglo-Saxon cemetery. The Gosforth Cross in Saint Mary's churchyard in Gosforth, Cumbria, Northern England, is a large stone cross that features carvings representing characters and scenes from Norse Mythology, including one of Thor fishing for the Jörmungandr, the Midgard Serpent. The sandstone cross was made in the 10th Century by the Vikings who settled there.

In Norse Mythology, Thor has two goats that pull his chariot across the skies. When he's hungry, he kills the goats and eats them, only to bring them back to life using his magical hammer, Mjölnir. Thor also used his hammer to cause thunder and lightning and to frighten away trolls. Amulets of Thunor's famous hammer have been found in female graves in Scandinavia, proving he was worshipped by men and women. They were also believed to frighten away trolls.

The Sun Cross Rune ᛡ was symbolic of thunder and represented Thunor in ancient times. Sword hilts engraved with Sun Crosses, dating to the 3rd Century, have been found in peat bogs in Denmark. It is important to remember that there were no Danes in Denmark at that time; Denmark was home to the Angles and Jutes, before they settled in what would become England. A scabbard engraved with a Sun Cross and a Christian cross was found near the river Seine, in France, dating to the 7th Century.

Sun Crosses have also been found in Anglo-Saxon graves in England. The Anglo-Saxon ship burial found at Sutton Hoo, East Anglia, England, contained numerous items bearing the Sun Cross. The Sun Cross is clearly marked on a hilt and sword belt found at Bifrons in Bekesbourne, Kent, in a grave dating to the 6th Century. An urn engraved with Sun Crosses was found at North Elmham, Norfolk, East Anglia. Scholar, Hilda Ellis Davidson, believed the Sun Cross must have held special significance as a funerary symbol.

'We have many examples of the swastika symbol
from Anglo-Saxon graves of the Pagan period,
with particular prominence on cremation urns
from the cemeteries of East Anglia.
On some of these, to be seen in the Cambridge Museum
of Archaeology and Ethnology,
it is depicted with such care and art
that it must surely have possessed
special significance as a funeral symbol.'

'The cult of Thor was linked up with men's habitation and possessions,
and with well-being of the family and community.
This included the fruitfulness of the fields, and Thor, although pictured
primarily as a storm god in the myths, was also concerned with the
fertility and preservation of the seasonal round.
In our own times, little stone axes from the distance past
have been used as fertility symbols
and placed by the farmer in the holes made by the drill
to receive the first seed of spring.
Thor's marriage with Sif of the golden hair,
about which we hear little in the myths,
seems to be a memory of the ancient symbol of divine marriage
between sky god and earth goddess,
when he comes to earth in the thunderstorm and the storm brings the rain
which makes the fields fertile.
In this way Thor, as well as Odin, may be seen to continue the cult of the
sky god which was known in the Bronze Age.'

Hilda Ellis Davidson

Frīge

The Norse Goddess, Frīgg, the wife of Odin and Goddess of love, peace, marriage and fertility, was worshipped by the English under the name Frīge. In England, Frīge gave her name to Friday, from the Old English 'Frīgedæg', meaning 'Frīge's Day'. For this reason it was considered good luck to marry on a Friday. Frīge was connected to the fate of men and wove the clouds with her famous spinning wheel. Her spinning wheel is remembered today and represented by Christmas wreaths.

A 10th Century manuscript found in Merseburg, Germany, features a Pagan invocation about how to heal a horse, known as the Second Merseburg Incantation. The name Phol is thought to be a byname for the Norse God, Baldr/Baldur.

The Second Merseburg Incantation

'Phol and Wōden travelled to the forest.
Then was for Baldur's foal its foot wrenched.
Then encharmed it Sindgund and Sunna, her sister,
then encharmed it Frija and Volla her sister,
then encharmed it Wōden, as he the best could,
as the bone-wrench, so for the blood wrench, and so the limb-wrench
bone to bone, blood to blood,
limb to limb, so be glued.'

Frīge was also known to the Long-beards, a Germanic Clan who founded the Kingdom of the Lombards, in Italy, 568-814.

'The Winnili then, having departed from Scandinavia with their leaders, Ibor and Aio, and coming into the region which is called Scoringa, settled there for some years. At that time, Ambri and Assi, leaders of the Vandals, were coercing all the neighbouring tribes by war. Already elated by many victories, they sent messengers to the Winnili to tell them that they should either pay tribute to the Vandals or make ready for the struggles of war. Then Ibor and Aio, with the approval of their mother, Gambara, determine that it is better to maintain liberty by arms than to stain it by the payment of tribute. They sent word to the Vandals by messengers that they would rather fight than be slaves. The Winnili were then all in the flower of their youth, but were very few in number since they had been only the third part of one island of no great size.'

> Historia gentis Langobardorum,
> (History of the Long-beards)
> Paul the Deacon, 720-799 A. D.

Frīge and her husband Wōden (Godan) are mentioned in the 7th Century work, Origo Gentis Langobardorum:

> 'When it became bright and the sun was rising, Frea, Godan's wife,
> turned the bed around where her husband was lying
> and put his face toward the east, and awakened him.
> And as he looked he saw the Winnili and their wives,
> and how their hair hung about their faces.
> And he said: "Who are these long beards?"
> Then spoke Frea to Godan:
> 'My lord, thou hast given them the name,
> now give them also the victory.'"

Sunna

The Anglo-Saxon Sunna gave her name to Sunday, from the Old English 'Sunnandæg', meaning 'Day of the Sun'. Sunna is the sister of Mōna, the personification of the Moon. In Norse Mythology, Sól (Sunna) rides a great horse-drawn chariot across the heavens and is continuously chased by the wolf, Sköll, that wishes to devour her. There isn't much written about Sunna in Old English, but she is mentioned in the Anglo-Saxon Rune Poem:

> ᚻ The sun is ever a joy in the hopes of seafarers
> when they journey away over the fishes' bath,
> until the courser of the deep bears them to land.'

Mōna

The Anglo-Saxon Mōna gave his name to Monday, from the Old English 'Mōnandæg', meaning 'Day of the Moon'. Mōna was also the guardian of the seasons, which gives us the name 'month', from the Old English 'mōnaþ'.

> 'In olden (Pagan) times, the English people
> - for it did not seem fitting
> that I should speak of other nations' observance of the year
> and yet be silent about my own nation's -
> calculated their months according to the course of the Moon.
> Hence, after the manner of the Greeks and the Romans,
> the months take their name from the Moon,
> for the Moon is called Mōna and the month monath (mōnaþ).'

The Venerable Bede, The Reckoning of Time, 673-735

Mōna is the brother of Sunna. In Norse Mythology, Máni (Mōna) is the male personification of the Moon who crosses the sky in a horse-drawn chariot, pursued by the great wolf, Hati, meaning 'He Who Hates'. From this we get the term 'The Man in the Moon'.

In Norse Mythology, at Ragnarök (The Fate of the Gods), the wolves catch and kill Sól and Máni, giving rise to natural disasters and the end of the world as we know it. The stars will disappear; the earth and mountains will shake so violently that the trees will come loose from the soil; the mountains will topple, and all restraints will break, causing Fenrir the giant wolf to break free from his bonds. The great serpent, Jörmungandr, whose coils hold in the sea, will breach land and spray venom onto land and sea. At the same time, Fenrir will kill Odin, and Thor will kill the serpent before dying from its poison.

'The customs of the Germani differ much from the Gauls.
They have no Druids to preside over sacred offices,
nor do they pay great regard to sacrifices.
The only beings they recognise as gods are things that they can see
and obviously benefit from, such as the sun, moon, and fire;
the other gods they have not even heard of.'

Julius Caesar, The Conquest of Gaul, 1st Century A. D.

Tīw

The Norse God, Týr, was worshipped by the English under the name Tīw, God of justice. In England, Tīw gave his name to Tuesday, from the Old English 'Tīwesdæg', meaning 'Tīw's Day'. Tuesley in Surrey, England, is named after him, from the Old English 'Tīwes Lēah', meaning 'Tīw's Clearing'. Tewin in Hertfordshire means 'Tīw's Meadow'. Tysoe in Warwickshire is also named after Tīw, from the Old English 'Tīwes Hōh', meaning 'Tīw's spur of land'. At Tysoe on Edge Hill, a red horse was cut on the hill slope and was scoured every Palm Sunday until the end of the 18th Century. It is likely that the horse represented the cult of Tīw. Tīw is mentioned in the Anglo-Saxon Rune Poem:

' ↑ Tīw is a guiding star;
well does it keep faith with princes;
it is ever on its course over the mists of night and never fails.'

Ing

The Anglo-Saxon God, Ing, is an old God. As we know, the English people are descended from the Anglo-Saxons. The ancestors of the Anglo-Saxons, who lived along the North Sea coast, were known to the Romans as the Ingaevones, the People of Ing, as first recorded by Cornelius Tacitus:

> 'In their ancient songs,
> their only form of recorded history,
> the Germani celebrate the earth-born god, Tuisto
> (possibly a reference to Tīw).
> They assign to him a son, Mannus,
> the founder of their race;
> and to Mannus three sons,
> after whom the people nearest the Ocean are named
> Ingaevones, those of the centre Herminones (Irminones),
> the remainder Istvaeones.'

The Anglo-Saxons worshipped Ing during the Winter festival of Yule (Christmas), sacrificing a wild boar, before eating its flesh in his honour. The boar was known as the Yule Boar and pre-dates the turkey by many centuries, maybe even thousands of years. As well as Yule, Ing is associated with agriculture and the weather. He bestows peace and pleasure upon mortals and was often depicted with a large erect penis, (as seen on the rock carving dating to the Bronze Age when the Angles still lived in what is now Denmark) and was probably a fertility God.

Ing is the oldest of his names, others include Yngvi, Frey and Freyr. The name 'Frey' means 'Lord'. The ancient Kingdom of Frīsia or Frīesland, in the Netherlands, is named after Frey, meaning 'Frey's land'. The ancient Swedish Clan known as The Ynglings claimed descent from Yngvi. In Norse Mythology, Frey is Freya's brother. The Norse Freya and the English Frīge are believed to be one and the same.

The boar represents Ing and symbolises protection, strength, ferocity and determination; qualities the wearer would adopt in battle and during the hunt. The Anglo-Saxon poem, Bēowulf, mentions warriors wearing boar-crested helms:

> 'Boar figures shone above cheek-protectors,
> adorned with gold, colourful and fire-hardened;
> each watched over life for the battle-brave men.'

> 'It was of beaten gold, princely headgear hooped and hasped
> by a weapon-smith who had worked wonders in days gone by
> and adorned it with boar-shapes; since then it had resisted every sword.'

Boar-crested war-helms, with long black bristles, have been found in Anglo-Saxon cemeteries, such as the Benty Grange helmet in Derbyshire, and many others.

> 'At this point our real knowledge of the world ends.
> However, turning to the right shore of the Suebian Sea (Baltic Sea),
> we find it washing the territories of the Aestii,
> who have the religion and general customs of the Suebi,
> but a language approximating to the British.
> They worship the Mother of the gods.
> They wear, as emblem of this cult, the masks of boars,
> which stand them in stead of armour or human protection
> and ensure the safety of the worshipper,
> even among his enemies.'
>
> Germania,
> Cornelius Tacitus, 9 A. D.

The legendary Germanic hero, Arminius, the hero of the Battle of the Teutoburg Forest, had an uncle called Inguiomer, possibly named after Ing. In the Bēowulf poem, King Hrōthgār is described as a descendant of Ing:

> 'Then the Danish Prince, descendant of Ing,
> handed over both the arms and the horses,
> urging Bēowulf to do well.'

The Anglo-Saxon Rune Poem contains these lines:

> ᛝ Ing was first amongst the East Danes
> so seen, until he went eastward over the sea.
> His wagon ran after.
> Thus the Heardings named that hero.

Ing is also the native English word for 'son', and is found in many English surnames and place-names in England.

Seaxnēat

The Anglo-Saxon God Seaxnēat or Saxnōt is recorded in the genealogies of the Kings of Essex, who placed Seaxnēat at its apex. It was later modified to make Seaxnēat the son of Wōden. It is likely that the famous Anglo-Saxon seax, a machete-like weapon, and the Saxons themselves, are named after Seaxnēat.

The Old Saxon Baptismal Vow, dating to the 9th Century, found in a monastery library in Mainz, Germany, mentions Seaxnēat by name:

> 'Do you renounce the devil?
> Responder: I renounce the devil.
> And all devil worship?
> Responder: And I renounce all devil worship.
> And all the deeds and words of the devil?
> Responder: And I renounce all the deeds and words of the devil, Thunear, Wōden, and Saxnōt,
> and all those fiends that are their companions.
> Do you believe in God, the Almighty Father?
> Responder: I believe in God, the Almighty Father.
> Do you believe in Christ, the son of God?
> Responder: I believe in Christ, the son of God.
> Do you believe in the Holy Spirit?
> Responder: I believe in the Holy Spirit.'

Hrēþe

The Anglo-Saxon Goddess, Hrethe, from the Old English 'Hrēþe', gave her name to Rhedmonth, from the Old English 'Hrēþmōnaþ'. Her name means bright, fierce, rough, famous or victorious, and she was connected with the month of March. Bēowulf's grandfather, King Hrēðel of the Gēats, may be named after Hrēþe, perhaps a fertility Goddess. Not much is known about Hrēþe, as she is attested solely by the Northumbrian monk and scholar, the Venerable Bede, in his 8th Century work, De temporum ratione:

> 'Hrēþmōnaþ is named for their goddess Hrēþe,
> to whom they sacrificed at this time.'

In Germany, she is known as Hertha. It is said that the Pagans of Germany would build an altar inside the hearth. Hertha would follow the smoke and come down the chimney to reward the good with gifts or punish the bad. She is the reason why we hang stockings over the fireplace at Christmas, to collect gifts during the Winter Solstice celebrations. The term 'hearth' comes from Hertha.

Ēastre

The Anglo-Saxon Goddess of rebirth and fertility, Ēastre, gave her name to the celebration of Easter. In Germany, she was known as Ostara. Ēastre means 'to shine'. In modern English, the word 'east' derives from this root, because the Sun rises in the east. Interestingly, one of the most numerous amulets found in female Anglo-Saxon graves is the cowrie shell, which may be a fertility symbol due to the underside resembling a vagina. The cowrie shells are native to the Red Sea in the Middle East and must have been brought to England by traders. Not much is known about Ēastre as she is attested solely by the Northumbrian monk and scholar, Bede. Bede states that during Ēastremōnaþ (Easter Month), the Pagan Anglo-Saxons held feasts in Ēastre's honour, but this tradition had died out by his time and was replaced by the Christian Paschal month, a celebration of the resurrection of Jesus. The worship of Ēastre is connected to the Spring Equinox, which marks the beginning of Spring (Summer to the Anglo-Saxons as they only had two seasons, Summer and Winter).

'Eosturmonath has a name which is now translated "Paschal month",
and which was once called after a goddess of theirs named Eostre,
in whose honour feasts were celebrated in that month.
Now they designate that Paschal season by her name,
calling the joys of the new rite by the time-honoured name
of the old observance.'

The Venerable Bede, 673-735

In the Gylfaginning, written in Old Norse by Snorri Sturluson, Jacob Grimm notes that there is a male being called Austri, who Jacob describes as a 'spirit of light'. Jacob says that a feminine version of the name would have been 'Austra', yet that the High German and Saxon peoples seem to have only formed Ostarâ and Eástre, feminine, and not Ostaro and Eástra, masculine.

'Ostara, Eástre seems therefore to have been the divinity
of the radiant dawn, of up-springing light,
a spectacle that brings joy and blessing,
whose meaning could be easily adapted by the resurrection day
of the Christians' God.
Bonfires were lit at Easter and,
according to popular belief of long standing,
the moment the sun rises on Easter Sunday morning,
he gives three joyful leaps.

> Water drawn on the Easter morning is,
> like that at Christmas, holy and healing.
> Here also heathen notions seems to have grafted
> themselves on great Christian festivals.
> Maidens clothed in white, who at Easter,
> at the season of returning spring,
> show themselves in clefts of the rock and on mountains,
> are suggestive of the ancient goddess.' - Jacob Grimm

Today, the celebration of Easter in Northern Europe is associated with hares and rabbits. Writing in the late 19th Century, Charles J. Billson had a theory connecting these customs and the worship of Ēostre. Charles wrote:

> '...whether there was a goddess named Eostre, or not,
> and whatever connection the hare may have had
> with the ritual of Saxon or British worship,
> there are good grounds for believing that the sacredness of this animal
> reaches back into an age still more remote,
> where it is probably a very important part
> of the great Spring Festival
> of the prehistoric inhabitants of this island.'

In English place-names, Ēastre may have given her name to Austerfield near Bawtry in the West Riding of Yorkshire, Eastry in Kent, Eastrea in Cambridgeshire, and Eastrington in the East Riding of Yorkshire. The Old English name, Easterwine, is also named after Ēastre. The female sex hormone, Oestrogen (Estrogen in the USA) is named after the Anglo-Saxon Goddess, Ēastre.

The Wyrd Sisters

In William Shakespeare's Macbeth, Shakespeare refers to the three witches as 'the Weird Sisters', who deliberately manipulate Macbeth to murder his way to the Scottish throne. Today, thanks to Shakespeare's use of the term 'weird', we now use it to describe anything odd, different, strange or peculiar. I believe this is due to a misunderstanding by Shakespeare's readers. I believe Shakespeare was using the old English concept of 'Wyrd' to describe the witches, meaning they are 'weavers of fate.'

The term 'Wyrd' is an Old English feminine noun, meaning 'the weaving of destiny or fate'. It may also be an Anglo-Saxon name for one of the three Goddesses found across Europe and are often referred to as the Norns. The term 'Wyrd' is derived from the Old English 'weorþan', 'to

become' or 'to turn'. The Wyrd Sisters were the weavers of fate, their tapestry is known today as the great Web of Wyrd. With each new thread brings forth new life. To sever a thread is to bring forth someone's death. Though considered ugly in William Shakespeare's famous play, in pre-Christian times the Wyrd Sisters were considered very beautiful.
In Norse Mythology, the three sisters sit by the Well of Wisdom and spin the great Web of Wyrd. Wyrd is the destiny of all things, a fate that cannot be changed, except by an extraordinary effort.

'Wyrd oft neroð unfægne eorl þonne his ellen dēah.'

'Fate often saves an undoomed hero as long as his courage is good.'

The Anglo-Saxon poem, Bēowulf

The Old English names for the Wyrd Sisters have been lost, but their Norse names have been preserved in Old Norse literature. The first sister in Old Norse is called Urðr, the Old Norse equivalent of Wyrd, 'that which has become'. The second is called Verðandi and is related to the Anglo-Saxon 'weorþan', 'that which is in the process of becoming'. The third is called Skuld, 'that which should be necessary'.

The concept of Wyrd is mentioned in various Old English poems, including Bēowulf and The Wanderer:

'Gæð a wyrd swa hio scel!'

'Fate goes ever as she shall!'

'Þær wæs symbla cyst, druncon wīn weras;
wyrd ne cūþon, geōsceaft grimme,
swā hit āgangen wearð eorla manegum,
syþðan æfen cwōm.'

'Men were drinking wine at that rare feast;
how could they know fate,
the grim shape of things to come?'

Bēowulf

'Wyrd bið ful aræd'

'Fate remains wholly inexorable'

> 'Ne mæg werigmod wyrde wiðstondan,
> ne se hreo hyge helpe gefremman.
> For ðon domgeorne dreorigne oft
> in hyra breostcofan bindað fæste.'
>
> 'A weary mood won't withstand wyrd,
> nor may the troubled mind find help.
> Often, therefore, the fame-yearners
> bind dreariness fast in their breast-coffins.'
>
> The Wanderer

In England and Germany, spinning or weaving has always been considered a task set for women and has very old, supernatural roots. Spinning was also important to the German Goddesses, Holda and Perchta (see Folklore). In Anglo-Saxon times, a woman who married a man in order to create peace between two families or clans was known as a peace-weaver, from the Old English 'friðuwebbe' (frithuwebbe); this no doubt comes from the Wyrd Sisters weaving the fabric of mankind. The Wyrd Sisters are the supernatural weavers of mankind, while mortal women are weavers of the fabric of society and keepers of the household and the family. Today, in England, a single, older woman is known as a spinster.

Nerthuz

Nerthuz is an Anglo-Saxon fertility Goddess. Unfortunately, we don't know much about her, but her name does survive in ancient literature.

'The Langabardi (Long-beards) are distinguished by the fewness of their numbers. Ringed round as they are by many mighty clans, they find safety, not in submission, but in battle and its perils. After them come the Reudigni (Rondings), Auiones (Eowan), Angli (Angles/English), Varni (Wærne), Eudoses (Jutes), Suarines, and Nuithones (Teutons), well-guarded by rivers and forests. There is nothing remarkable about these clans, unless it is the common worship of Nerthuz or Earth Mother. They believe she is interested in human affairs and drives a sleigh amongst them. On an island of the sea stands a sacred grove, and in the grove a consecrated sleigh, veiled with a cloth, which none but the priest may touch. The priest can feel the presence of the goddess in this holy of holies, and attends her with the deepest reverence as her sleigh is drawn along by cows. The following days are filled with rejoicing and merry-making in every place that she has visited and entertained. No one goes to war, no one takes up arms; every iron object is locked away. Then, and then only, are peace and quiet known and welcomed, until the goddess, when she has had enough of the society of men, is restored to her sacred precinct by the priest. After that, the sleigh, the cloth, and the goddess herself, are cleansed in a secluded lake. This service is performed by slaves who are immediately drowned in the lake. Thus mystery begets terror and a pious reluctance to ask what that sight can be that is only seen by men who are doomed to die.'

Germania,
Cornelius Tacitus, 9 A. D.

Valkyries

The term 'Valkyrie' comes from the Old English 'Wælcyrie' and 'Wælcyrge', which appear in several Old English manuscripts. It is debated whether the terms come from Anglo-Saxon Paganism or were influenced by the Vikings and the Old Norse 'Valkyrja', plural 'valkyrjur', meaning 'chooser(s) of the slain'.

In the 11th Century Anglo-Saxon sermon, Sermo Lupi ad Anglos, Bishop Wulfstān II, wrote a list of evil beings, including Valkyries, witches and harlots. For Valkyries, he used the Old English 'wælcyrian':

> '...myltestran] bearnmyrðran] fule forlegene horingas manage,]
> ...wiccan] wælcyrian.'

> '...harlots and child-murderers and many foul, perverted whoremongers and witches and slain choosers.'

The 11th Century manuscript, Aldhelm's De laudis virginitatis, refers to a Wælcyrge as a Goddess. In Old English literature, the term 'Wælcyrge' is also used to describe the Greek Furies, the Goddesses of Vengeance in Greek Mythology.

It is debatable whether the Valkyries were Goddesses or not, but they were certainly supernatural female figures who chose those who are worthy to die in battle and join Wōden in the afterlife. Once in Valhalla, the Hall of the Slain, the Valkyries performed the duty of the ealu bora, the ale bearer, and poured the fallen warriors their drinks. In Anglo-Saxon society, it was a Queen's role to be the ealu bora and ritually pour the noblemen their drinks. Women have been associated with brewing ale since ancient Mesopotamia, one of the oldest civilisations in the world. In England they were known as alewives.

Other terms for Valkyries in Old Norse sources include 'Óskmey', meaning 'wish maid' and 'Óðins meyjar', meaning 'Odin's maids'. Valkyries were also associated with ravens, a symbol of Wōden, because ravens often visit battlefields to feast from the flesh of the dead. In Norse literature, the Valkyries are described as beautiful and white-skinned and are often depicted wearing long eagle-feathered war-helmets.

> 'The ring-giver saw them riding,
> a snapping of swords must happen,
> it's come, the grey spears' greeting
> as the Gods ride fast through the pasture.
> Odin exults to see
> the Valkyries eager for battle,
> those Goddesses dripping forth gore
> drenching the lives of men.'
>
> The Icelandic Viga-Glúm Saga, 13th Century

In 1324, in Bergen, Norway, there was a witch trial involving Ragnhild Tregagás, who used a charm to invoke the Valkyrie, Göndul, in order to end her marriage to her husband:

> 'I send out from me the spirits of the Valkyrie, Göndul.
> May the first bite you in the back.
> May the second bite you in the breast.
> May the third turn hate and envy upon you.'

Ragnhild was found guilty and was sentenced to strict fasting and a seven-year-long pilgrimage to holy places outside of Norway.
There are two Old English charms that mention female figures that may represent the Anglo-Saxon notion of Valkyries. One is the Wið færstice, a charm to cure a sudden pain or stitch:

> 'Against a sudden stitch,
> take feverfew and the red nettle that grows in the house,
> and waybread; boil in butter.
> Loud they were, oh! they were loud,
> when they rode over the burial-mound; they were resolute,
> when they rode over the land.
> Shield yourself now, you can survive this attack.
> Out, little spear, if it is in here!
> I stood under linden, under the light shield,
> where the mighty women considered
> their power, and they threw shrieking spears;
> I will throw another one back again,
> a flying spear right back toward them.
> Out, little spear, if it is in here!
> A smith sat and hammered a little knife,

an iron wondrously strong.
Out, little spear, if it is in here!
Six smiths sat and made a deadly spear.
Out, spear! Not in, spear!
If there is any iron in here, the work of a witch, it will dissolve.
If you were shot in the skin or were shot in the flesh
or were shot in the blood or were shot in a joint,
let your life never be injured.
If it was the shot of devils, or it was the shot of elves
or it was the shot of a witch, now I will help you.
This help to you for the shot of devils,
this help to you for the shot of elves,
this help to you for the shot of a witch; I will help you.
Fly there to the mountain's head.
Be whole: God help you.
Then take the knife and put it into the liquid.'

The second charm is called For a Swarm of Bees; a charm to keep honey bees from swarming:

'Take earth with your right hand
and throw it under your right foot, saying:
I've got it, I've found it:
Lo, earth masters all creatures,
it masters evil, it masters deceit,
it masters humanity's greedy tongue.
Throw light soil over them (the bees) as they swarm, saying:
Sit, victory women, settle on earth:
never in fear fly to the woods.
Please be mindful of my welfare as all men are of food and land.'

Based on the evidence, I believe the Anglo-Saxons knew of the Valkyries long before the coming of the Vikings and worshipped them as Goddesses, associating them with the fate of brave men upon England's battlefields, before taking the chosen warriors to the afterlife, to feast and drink with Wōden; the highest a mortal man can achieve.

Ides

The most mysterious supernatural female beings found in Anglo-Saxon and Germanic Paganism are the Idisi, singular Idis or Ides. They are referred to as Valkyries, Goddesses, monstrous hell-brides and well-respected and dignified women. The term 'Ides' is used in the Old English poem, Bēowulf:

>'Grendles mōdor, ides āglæc-wīf yrmþe gemunde.'

>'Grendel's mother, monstrous hell-bride, brooded on her wrongs.'

In Old Saxon the Ides are called Idis. In Old High German they are known as Itis and mean 'well-respected and dignified woman'. There is a 10th Century manuscript found in Merseburg, Germany, that features a Pagan invocation that refers to the Idisi; it is known as the The First Merseburg Charm:

>'Once the Idisi set forth,
>to this place and that;
>some fastened fetters;
>some hindered the horde,
>some loosed the bonds from the brave.
>Leap forth from the fetters!
>Escape from the foes!'

Scholars have theorized that the Idisi may be an alternative name for the Valkyries or the Norse Dísir; female beings associated with fate. In Norse Mythology, a Dís, plural Dísir, are ghosts or Goddesses associated with fate, who can either be good or bad. A sacrifice to the Dísir was called a Dísablót, and their veneration may derive from the worship of the spirits of the dead.

Interestingly, the place-name, Idistaviso, in Germany, means the 'meadow of the Idisi', or 'women's meadow'. In the year 16 A. D., The Battle of Idistaviso took place between Roman legions and an alliance of Germanic clans, commanded by the legendary Arminius. The battle marked the end of a three year series of campaigns by the Roman Emperor's nephew and heir, Germanicus. It is possible that the battle and the area were named due to the Idisi, perhaps made up of priestess-warriors, taking part in the battle.

Like the Valkyries, I believe the Ides were once worshipped as Goddesses by my ancestors. I believe, over time, Christian scholars have demonised them because they were Pagan and because they were women. If this is true, then that would mean that Grendel's mother from the Bēowulf poem wasn't the monster we have been led to believe. We must remember, the story of Bēowulf was passed down through the generations in the oral tradition, before it was written down by Christian monks, who wrote it for a Christian audience. The poem refers to the monster Grendel as a descendant of Cain from the Christian Bible, but what about the older traditions? Was Grendel's mother a Goddess who gave birth to a hideous monster, much like the Norse God, Loki, who fathered Hel, Fenrir and the World serpent? In the poem, Grendel's mother does nothing wrong and only acts out of revenge when her son is killed by Bēowulf. Is it possible that Grendel's mother could have once been a Goddess or a venerated water fairy or spirit, such as a Knucker?

Herne the Hunter

Herne the Hunter is a mysterious, ghostly figure in English folklore. He wears large deer antlers upon his head, rides a horse, torments cattle, and rattles chains. He is believed to haunt Windsor Forest and Great Park in the English county of Berkshire, near London. The earliest mention of Herne the Hunter comes from William Shakespeare's 1597 play, The Merry Wives of Windsor. But Shakespeare didn't invent the legend, and was writing about an existing legend:

> 'Sometime a keeper here in Windsor Forest,
> doth all the winter-time, at still midnight,
> walk round about an oak, with great ragg'd horns;
> and there he blasts the tree, and takes the cattle,
> and makes milk-kine yield blood, and shakes a chain
> in a most hideous and dreadful manner.
> You have heard of such a spirit, and well you know
> the superstitious idle-headed eld
> receiv'd, and did deliver to our age,
> this tale of Herne the Hunter for a truth.'

The Pagan Angles settled Windsor Forest in the early Middle Ages and brought with them their stories about Wōden. The name 'Herne' is derived from the title 'Herian', a title used for Wōden in his role as leader of fallen warriors.

The Concept of Frith

Frith, from the Old English 'friðuwebbe', is an interesting concept found in Anglo-Saxon paganism. Frith is to grow up amongst your own people, drink and feast with your own kind, to hear your native tongue spoken and to listen to the sagas of your ancestors. Frith is to know who you are and where you come from. It is the peace of mind in knowing that your people will continue long after you have left this realm.

The Anglo-Saxon Rune Poem
(in Modern English)

ᚠ Wealth is a comfort to all men;
yet must every man bestow it freely,
if he wishes to gain honour in the sight of the Lord.

ᚢ The aurochs is proud and has great horns;
it is a very savage beast and fights with its horns;
a great ranger of the moors, it is a creature of mettle.

ᚦ The thorn is exceedingly sharp,
an evil thing for any warrior to touch,
uncommonly severe on all who sit among them.

ᚪ The mouth is the source of all language,
a pillar of wisdom and a comfort to wise men,
a blessing and a joy to every warrior.

ᚱ Riding seems easy to every warrior while he is indoors
and very courageous to him who travels the high-roads
on the back of a stout horse.

ᚳ The torch is known to every living man by its pale, bright flame;
it always burns where princes sit within.

ᚷ Generosity brings credit and honour, which support one's dignity;
it furnishes help and subsistence
to all broken men who are devoid of aught else.

ᚹ Bliss he enjoys who knows not suffering, sorrow nor anxiety,
and has prosperity and happiness and a good enough house.

ᚻ Hail is the whitest of grain;
it is whirled from the vault of heaven
and is tossed about by gusts of wind
and then it melts into water.

ᚾ Trouble is oppressive to the heart;
yet often it proves a source of help and salvation
to the children of men, to everyone who heeds it betimes.

ᛁ Ice is very cold and immeasurably slippery;
it glistens as clear as glass and most like to gems;
it is a floor wrought by the frost, fair to look upon.

ᛄ Summer is a joy to men, when God, the holy King of Heaven,
suffers the earth to bring forth shining fruits
for rich and poor alike.

ᛇ The yew is a tree with rough bark,
hard and fast in the earth, supported by its roots,
a guardian of flame and a joy upon an estate.

ᛈ Peorth is a source of recreation and amusement to the great,
where warriors sit blithely together in the banqueting hall.

ᛉ The Eolh-sedge is mostly to be found in a marsh;
it grows in the water and makes a ghastly wound,
covering with blood every warrior who touches it.

ᛊ The sun is ever a joy in the hopes of seafarers
when they journey away over the fishes' bath,
until the courser of the deep bears them to land.

ᛏ Tīw is a guiding star;
well does it keep faith with princes;
it is ever on its course over the mists of night and never fails.

ᛒ The poplar bears no fruit; yet without seed it brings forth suckers,
for it is generated from its leaves.
Splendid are its branches and gloriously adorned
its lofty crown which reaches to the skies.

ᛖ The horse is a joy to princes in the presence of warriors.
A steed in the pride of its hoofs,
when rich men on horseback bandy words about it;
and it is ever a source of comfort to the restless.

ᛗ The joyous man is dear to his kinsmen;
yet every man is doomed to fail his fellow,
since the Lord by his decree will commit the vile carrion to the earth.

ᛚ The ocean seems interminable to men,
if they venture on the rolling bark
and the waves of the sea terrify them
and the courser of the deep heed not its bridle.

ᛝ Ing was first amongst the East Danes
so seen, until he went eastward
over the sea. His wagon ran after.
Thus the Heardings named that hero.

ᛟ An estate is very dear to every man,
if he can enjoy there in his house
whatever is right and proper in constant prosperity.

ᛞ Day, the glorious light of the Creator, is sent by the Lord;
it is beloved of men, a source of hope and happiness to rich and poor,
and of service to all.

ᚪ The oak fattens the flesh of pigs for the children of men.
Often it traverses the gannet's bath,
and the ocean proves whether the oak keeps faith
in honourable fashion.

ᚫ The ash is exceedingly high and precious to men.
With its sturdy trunk it offers a stubborn resistance,
though attacked by many a man.

ᚣ Yr is a source of joy and honour to every prince and warrior;
it looks well on a horse and is a reliable equipment for a journey.

ᛡ Iar is a river fish and yet it always feeds on land;
it has a fair abode encompassed by water, where it lives in happiness.

ᛠ The grave is horrible to every warrior,
when the corpse quickly begins to cool
and is laid in the bosom of the dark earth.
Prosperity declines, happiness passes away
and covenants are broken.

Part Two
The Anglo-Saxon Calendar

Latin	Old English	Modern English
January	Æftera Geola	After Yule
January-February	Wulfmōnaþ	Wolf Month
February	Sōlmōnaþ	Month of Hearthcakes
March	Hrēþmōnaþ	Hrethe's Month
April	Ēastremōnaþ	Ēastre Month
May	þrimilcimōnaþ	Three Milkings
June	Ærra Liða	Going before Summer
July	Æftera Liða	Midsummer
August	Weōdmōnaþ	Weed Month
September	Hāliġmōnaþ	Holy Month
	(Hærvestmōnaþ)	(Harvest Month)
October	Winterfylleþ	Winter Full Moon
November	Blótmōnaþ	Sacrifice Month
December	Ærra Geola	Going before Yule
Christmas	Geol	Yule
Nativity	Mōdraniht	Mothers' Night

Æftera Geola

January was known as Æftera Geola, the month after Yule. It was an important time when farmers would spread the ashes from the Yule Log onto their fields to assure new crops in the coming year. Many pagan celebrations were also carried out to assure the fertility of the land, such as Molly Dancing, the Whittlesea Straw Bear Festival, and many others (see Folk Dancers and Pagan Traditions).

Wulfmōnaþ

January-February was also known as the Wolf Month, from the Old English 'Wulfmōnaþ'. The Wolf Month was the first full month of wolf hunting by the Anglo-Saxon nobility. Galfrid the monk, writing about the miracles of Saint Cuthbert, seven centuries earlier, said that wolves were so numerous in Northumbria that it was virtually impossible for even the richest flock masters to protect their sheep, despite employing many men for the job. The Norman Kings employed servants as wolf hunters and gave them land in exchange for hunting and killing wolves. William the Conqueror granted the lordship of Riddesdale in Northumberland to Robert de Umfraville on condition that he defended that land from enemies and wolves. Officially, the hunting season would end on March 25th, so it would include the cubbing season, when wolves were at their most vulnerable and their fur was of greater quality.

Sōlmōnaþ

February was Sōlmōnaþ, the Month of Hearthcakes, when ritual offerings of savoury cakes and loaves of bread were offered to the Gods to ensure a good year's harvest. The name was recorded by Bede in his work, The Reckoning of Time:

> 'Sōlmōnaþ can be said to be the month of cakes, which were offered to their gods.'

Hrēþmōnaþ

March was Hrēþmōnaþ, the Month of Hrēþe, named after a fertility Goddess. It was also the last month of Winter and the end of the wolf hunting season. It was a time to bake cakes and offer them to the Gods to help bring forth Summer. (see Hrēþe)

Ēastremōnaþ

April was Ēastremōnaþ, the Month of Ēastre, named after the Goddess of rebirth and fertility (see Ēastre). It was also the first month of Summer. It was a time to celebrate rebirth and renewal, when the land warms up and animals have their young; when the birds are singing in the trees and the natural world bursts into life. More importantly, it was a time of victory, when the Sun returned in full strength, and light had triumphed over darkness, and life had triumphed over death. Ēastremōnaþ marked the beginning of happier times.

þrimilcimōnaþ

May was the Month of Three Milkings, from the Old English 'þrimilcimōnaþ', when cows were so well-fed on fresh spring grass that they could be milked three times a day. þrimilcimōnaþ is also associated with the Pagan May Day celebrations. Bede wrote:

> 'The fifth month is called þrimilcimōnaþ in our language, because before, there was such abundance in Britain and also in Germania, whence the Angle people came to Britain, would milk their cows thrice a day.'

Ærra Liða and Æftera Liða

The month of June was known as Ærra Liða (before Litha). The month of July was known as Æftera Liða (after Litha). One of the most important annual events was the Summer Solstice, the longest day of the year. This event was so important that it was guarded by two Moons, Ærra Liða and Æftera Liða.

The celebration of Liða (Litha) was a celebration of life, when the Sun was at its strongest and most magical. It was also a celebration of light triumphing over darkness, and life triumphing over death. Animals were sacrificed to the Gods and thrown onto bonfires that were lit across the land next to holy wells and all sacred places, to protect the people against bad spirits. Liða and the Summer Solstice was a time of great healing and new life. As the Sun rose high in the sky, her shining light was believed to chase away goblins, wood-elves and dragons, and could turn trolls to stone.

In Germany, the Summer Solstice is called Sommersonnenwende. On June 20th, 1653, the Nuremberg town council issued the following order:

'Where experience herefore have shown, that after the old heathen use, on John's day in every year, in the country, as well in towns as villages, money and wood have been gathered by young folk, and there upon the so-called sonnenwendt or zimmet fire kindled, and thereat winebibbing, dancing about the said fire, leaping over the same, with burning of sundry herbs and flowers, and setting of brands from the said fire in the fields, and in many other ways all manner of superstitious work carried on. Council of Nürnberg town neither can nor ought to forbear to do away with all such unbecoming superstition, Paganism, and peril of fire on this coming day of St. John.'

Fires were extremely important in Anglo-Saxon times, and the celebration of Liða was certainly a fire festival. In olden times, bonfires were known as bone-fires, where animals had been sacrificed to the Gods, their flesh eaten and their bones thrown onto outdoor fires.
In England, from the 13th Century, Midsummer was celebrated on Midsummer's Eve (Saint John's Eve, June 23rd) and Saint Peter's Eve (June 28th), with the lighting of bonfires, feasting and merrymaking. In late 14th Century England, John Mirk of Lilleshall Abbey, Shropshire, gave the following description:

'At first, men and women came to church
with candles and other lights and prayed all night long.
In the process of time, however, men left such devotion
and used songs and dances and fell into lechery
and gluttony, turning the good, holy devotion into sin.'

The church fathers decided to put a stop to these practices and ordained that people should fast on the evening before, and thus turned waking into fasting. Mirk adds that at the time of his writing:

> '...in worship of St John the Baptist,
> men stay up at night and make three kinds of fires:
> one is of clean bones and no wood and is called a bonnefyre;
> another is of clean wood and no bones, and is called a wakefyre,
> because men stay awake by it all night;
> and the third is made of both bones and wood
> and is called St. John's fire.'

After the Reformation (the breaking away from the Catholic Church), other Midsummer festivities had poor relations with the Reformed establishment. The Chester Midsummer Watch Parade which begun in 1498 and was held at every Summer Solstice in years when the Chester Mystery Plays were not performed. Despite the cancellation of the plays in 1575, the parade continued. In 1599, the Lord Mayor ordered that the parades be banned and the costumes destroyed. The parade was permanently banned in 1675.

The raising and dancing around a Maypole during the Summer festivities is an old Pagan custom in England and Germany. In Germany, placing greenery over houses and barns were believed to bring good fortune and health to people and livestock. (see May Day)

Weōdmōnaþ

August was known as Weed Month, from the Old English 'Weōdmōnaþ', and was a time for planting crops. Bede writes:

> 'The month of August we call Weōdmōnaþ in our language,
> for these grow most in this month.'

Hāliġmōnaþ

September was known as Holy Month, from the Old English 'Hāliġmōnaþ' or Harvest Month, from the Old English 'Hærvestmōnaþ'.

> 'In the ninth month in the year there are thirty days.
> The month is called in Latin September,
> and in our language holy month,
> because our ancestors, when they were heathen,
> sacrificed to their idols in that month.'

The Anglo-Saxon poem, Menologium seu Calendarium Poeticum

Winterfylleþ

October was known as Winterfylleþ, the Winter Full Moon and the beginning of Winter. Bede writes:

> 'The old English people split the year into two seasons, summer and winter, placing six months - during which the days are longer than the nights - in summer, and the other six in winter. They called the month when the winter season began, Winterfylleþ, a word composed of "winter" and "full moon", because winter began on the first full moon of that month.'

Blótmōnaþ

November was known as the Month of Sacrifices, from the Old English 'Blōtmonath'. With the end of Summer, the Anglo-Saxons couldn't grow enough food to feed their entire livestock over the long Winter. The natural solution was to keep the animals that would survive the Winter in barns and to cull the remaining. Those that were chosen were then sacrificed to the Gods at Blōtmonath; a kindness, to save them from starvation and disease. A great feast would then follow at the Winter Solstice - this is the true origins of the Christmas dinner that we know today. The term 'blōt' is Old English for 'ritual sacrifice' and is similar to the Old Norse 'blót'. A blōt could be dedicated to any of the Anglo-Saxon Gods, the spirits of the land, and to the ancestors. The name was recorded by Bede:

> 'Blōtmonath is month of immolations (sacrifices), for it was in this month that the cattle which were to be slaughtered were dedicated to the gods.'

An entry in the Menologium seu Calendarium Poeticum reads:

> 'This month is called Novembris in Latin, and in our language the month of sacrifice (Blōtmonath), because our forefathers, when they were heathens, always sacrificed in this month, that is, that they took and devoted to their idols the cattle which they wished to offer.'

Yule

The word 'Yule' comes from the Old English 'Geola', meaning 'wheel'. To the Anglo-Saxons, Yule was the most important time of the year and was guarded by two Moons, Ærra Geola and Æftera Geola. December was known as Ærra Geola, the month before Yule. January was known as Æftera Geola, the month after Yule.

The Yuletide celebrations went hand in hand with the Winter Solstice, the shortest day and longest night of the year, when the veil between the living and the dead is thinnest and spirits can cross the threshold to return to their loved ones or to torment the living. Yule was later replaced by the Twelve Days of Christmas by Christians who found it impossible to eradicate this ancient Pagan tradition, though not from a lack of trying. In the 17th Century, Oliver Cromwell's Puritan government tried to ban Christmas because it was a Pagan holiday. There were riots across the country and Christmas church services were broken up by armed soldiers. Christmas decorations were pulled down and burned by the mayor of London. Even Christmas puddings were banned. Christmas was also banned in the British colonies in what would become the United States of America. One public notice read:

'The observation of Christmas having been deemed a sacrilege,
the exchange of gifts and greetings,
dressing in fine clothing, feasting and similar Satanical practices,
are hereby forbidden,
with the offender liable to a fine of five shillings.'

The celebration of Yule had nothing to do with Satanism, but it was a time of great superstition. It was a Pagan celebration of one cycle coming to an end and the start of another; a turning of the wheel; a time when the Sun leaves the realm of the living, allowing darkness and ice to cover the land, killing livestock, plants and crops. It was a supernatural fire festival, where candles and bonfires were lit to brighten up the dome of the sky, in defiance of the cold, dark Winter, and to frighten away bad spirits and malevolent fairies. It was a celebration when sacrifices were made to entice the Gods to bring back the Sun, the giver of life, the true saviour of mankind. The bones of the sacrificed animals (those who couldn't survive the Winter due to a lack of food) were thrown onto bonfires (bone-fires) and the flesh was eaten in a great feast.

In England there was the Blōtmonath, a great culling of livestock, to prevent them from starving through the Winter. Using salt and the cold weather, the meat was easily preserved until the Winter Solstice, where the people would enjoy a great feast. In Scandinavia, at the beginning of Winter, the lady of the household would make a blood sacrifice to the elves, called a Álfablót or Elven Sacrifice. It was a time when the crops had been harvested and the animals were fat and awaiting the Winter slaughter. It is likely that the sacrifices were connected to ancestors and fertility, a way to ensure the family was protected during the dark days of Winter. Elves are still associated with Christmas to this day and help Santa Claus prepare gifts for well-behaved children. Also in Scandinavia, there was the Midwinter sacrifice, known as the Dísablót, a great sacrifice to honour the Dísir, the spirits of female ancestors, which coincides with the Anglo-Saxon Mothers' Night.

As well as feasting, Yule was a time for gatherings and fellowship, gift-giving and toasting. The first toast was to Wōden, the second was to Ing (also known as Frey), and the third was to the king, wishing him good health and hæl. Like the Irish Samhain, an extra place was set at the table for dead relatives. Memorial toasts were then made in memory of departed kinsmen. Toasting is believed to have been brought to Britain by the Anglo-Saxons, who literally placed a piece of toasted bread in their drinks.

In Scandinavia, as the Winter Solstice approached, a boar, known as the Yule Boar, was chosen and sacrificed to Frey (Ing), God of peace, light and agriculture, in the hope he would bring back the Sun. Until the 17th Century, it was customary in England and Scandinavia to hunt wild boars, cut off its head and offer it to the God of agriculture.

'It was ancient custom that when sacrifice was to be made,
all farmers were to come to the heathen temple
and bring with them the food they needed while the feast lasted.
At this feast all were to take part in the drinking of ale.
All kinds of livestock were killed in connection with it,
horses also; and all the blood from them was called hlaut,
and hlautbolli, the vessel holding the blood;
and hlautteinar, the sacrificial twigs.
These were fashioned like sprinklers,
and were to be smeared all over with blood
the pedestals of the idols and also the walls of the temple
within and without;
and likewise the men present were to be sprinkled with blood.
But the meat of the animals was to be boiled
and served as food at the banquet.
Fires were to be lit in the middle of the temple floor,
and kettles hung over them.
The sacrificial beaker was to be borne around the fire,
and he who made the feast and was chieftain,
was to bless the beaker as well as all the sacrificial meat.'

Snorri Sturluson,
Heimskringla, 12th Century

The wild boar was the traditional meal at Yule until it was replaced by the peacock, roast beef, venison, goose, and finally the turkey in the 19th Century. In 21st Century England, the boar still has its place on the Christmas dinner table in the form of 'pigs in a blanket', pork sausages wrapped in bacon. Interestingly, the traditional Christmas pudding was, until quite recently, a bowl of porridge. It was also customary in England to leave out a bowl of porridge to appease the household fairies. This custom survives today, only we now leave out milk and cookies for Santa.

As mentioned earlier, it was customary in Scandinavia for children to fill old boots with hay for Odin's eight-legged horse when he visited during the Wild Hunt (see Wild Hunt). In exchange for the hay, Odin would leave a small gift as a thank you. Also, the German Goddess, Hertha, would come down people's chimneys to reward the good with gifts or punish the bad. She is the reason why we hang stockings over the fireplace on Christmas Eve.

In Pagan England, the day before the Winter Solstice was called Mothers' Night, from the Old English 'Mōdraniht'. Mothers' Night was a time when the English honoured the Goddesses, to bring peace and protection to their kith and kin, and when sons and daughters returned from the dead, dressed as Wolf-Coats and Swan-Maidens, to the embrace of their mothers and fathers (see Wolf-Coats, Werewolves and the Dog-Headed People).

'...began the year on the 8th Calends of January (25th December),
when we celebrate the birth of the Lord.
That very night, which we hold so sacred,
they used to call by the heathen word Mōdraniht,
that is, "mothers' night",
because, we suspect, of the ceremonies
they enacted all that night.'

The Venerable Bede, 673-735

The Anglo-Saxons, Scandinavians and Germans idolised trees, such as the Maypole, which is made from sacred birch trees, Thunor's Oak, Irminsul, and the giant yew ash at Uppsala.

'Near that temple is a very large tree with widespread branches
which are always green both in winter and summer.
What kind of tree it is nobody knows.
There is also a spring there where the Pagan are accustomed
to perform sacrifices and to immerse a human being alive.
As long as his body is not found,
the request of the people will be fulfilled.

The description of the tree and the location of a well nearby
are reminiscent of the evergreen, Yggdrasil,
which stood above the Well of Urd (Wyrd),
and it is possible that the Swedes consciously had created
a copy of the world of their Norse gods at Uppsala.'

Adam of Bremen
Gesta Hammaburgensis ecclesiae pontificum,
11th Century

'Svein, the King's brother-in-law,
remained behind in the assembly,
and offered the Swedes to do sacrifices on their behalf
if they would give him the Kingdom.
They all agreed to accept Svein's offer,
and he was then recognized as King over all Sweden.
A horse was then brought to the assembly and hewn in pieces
and cut up for eating, and the sacred tree was smeared with blood.
Then all the Swedes abandoned Christianity,
and sacrifices started again.
They drove King Ingi away;
and he went into Västergötland.'

Hervarar Saga, 13th Century

The worship of trees was once common and survives to this day with the great Christmas icon, the Christmas Tree. The Christmas Tree has nothing to do with Christianity or the Nativity, and is Pagan to its roots. Christmas Trees are usually conifers, spruce, pine or fir. When all plant life appears dead, only the evergreens remain alive, surviving between the world of the living and the world of the dead, and so they were believed to have magical properties. The Christmas Tree itself was a form of protection.

The Old English 'bēam' refers to trees and quite possibly to sacred trees. Anglo-Saxon place-names containing the word 'stapol', meaning post or pillar, may represent areas where sacred trees were once worshipped in England. Thurstable Hundred in Essex and Thurstaple in Kent were known in Anglo-Saxon times as 'Þunres stapol', meaning 'Thunor's Pillar'.

It is almost certain that trees dedicated to Thunor were worshipped in those areas; perhaps they had once been struck by lightning and thus blessed by the thunder God. An English folk custom involves the raising of a branch from a roof or chimney of a newly built house as a form of protection against lightning from the thunder God. In England, some houses have been built around large trees, known as 'luck trees', and were said to be linked to the family's luck and prosperity.

The decoration of trees, whether indoors or out, is an old Pagan custom. For thousands of years, people in Britain, Europe and all across the world have decorated trees outside their home and in the surrounding forests, until the Middle-Ages, where the custom of bringing Christmas Trees indoors began in Germany.

Though Yule was a time for family and to remember one's ancestors, it was also a time to fear, a time when bad spirits could cross the threshold and haunt the living. Today, we leave gifts under the Christmas Tree for our loved ones, but this ancient custom comes from leaving gifts of nuts and fruits under forest trees for the Land Wights, the good spirits that help protect the forest (see Wights). Interestingly, fruit and nuts have been found in Anglo-Saxon graves, possibly as gifts to the deceased or because of their association with the spirit world.

It was once customary in Scandinavia to decorate trees with runes, coloured clothes and food, to entice the tree spirits to come back in Summer. Animals were also taken out into the forest and sacrificed to the Gods, asking for protection and to bring back the Sun, before being hung from sacred trees. The red bulbs that we hang on Christmas Trees today represents droplets of blood dripping from the sacrificed livestock. Bells were also used to decorate the forest trees to frighten away bad spirits and fairies. In England, it is still customary to decorate Christmas Trees with bells. It is also customary to place a fairy on top of the tree, another form of protection from bad spirits. Another custom is to decorate Christmas Trees with silver tinsel, this is believed to represent dew-covered spider webs that once decorated outdoor trees.

It was once customary to place lit candles on Christmas Trees to frighten away bad spirits and fairies, but once the trees came indoors this proved too dangerous and has resulted in many deaths. Tree candles today are replaced with electric lights, known as fairy lights. Christmas Trees in the German town of Oberammergau are placed on graves alongside lit candles so the deceased can join in with the celebrations. In Bavaria, a lit candle is placed at every grave to honour the dead. Until the late 19th Century, English grocers gave their customers a complimentary pair of enormous Yule Candles as a free Christmas present; one blue, the other red. They were lit and extinguished only by the head of the household. The Yule Candle, wreathed in protective greenery, was placed in the centre of the table on Christmas Day and would burn all night until the following morning. It was believed that if the candle burnt out or was put out before the morning, death would follow.

In England today, flame-lit candles are placed in the centre of the table during the Christmas dinner and are often used as Christmas decorations. In more recent times, electric candles are used to decorate windowsills and on top of fireplaces.

Other forms of protection include the use of evergreens, such as mistletoe, ivy and holly. As the Winter Solstice, the Night of the Dead, approaches, plants and vegetation begin to die and rot, leaves fall from trees and the tree itself appears to be dead. Because evergreens don't die at this time, they were believed to live between the world of the living and the dead. They were seen as magical and were used to protect people's homes, the communal hall and the surrounding forest. This is the origins of our Christmas decorations.

> 'Down with the rosemary and so
> down with the bais and mistletoe,
> down with the holly, ivy, all
> wherewith you drest the Christmas hall.
> That so the superstitious find
> not one least branch there left behind,
> for look, how many leaves there be,
> neglected there, maids trust to me,
> so many goblins you shall see.'
>
> John Stow
> Survey of London, 1598

Mistletoe is native to Britain and Europe and ripens in December. Since pre-Christian times, it has been used to heal certain ailments. The ancient Greeks used it for countless diseases, but also for menstrual cramps and spleen disorders. They also believed it was an aphrodisiac and could cause eternal life. In Greek myth, Zeus' daughter, Persephone, opened the gates of Hades using mistletoe berries. In ancient Rome, it was used in a balm to help with epilepsy and ulcers. Druids once used it to help restore fertility and believed it provided protection from evil.

It is an English tradition to hang a branch of mistletoe over the doorway of one's home for peace and good luck. In the 18th Century, this custom led to mistletoe becoming associated with Christmas. Also in England, it was a folk custom for young girls to take a mistletoe leaf and put it under their pillow at night. They would then dream about a particular person they wanted to marry. Mistletoe is also hung in one's home as the New Year approaches, and the previous year's mistletoe is taken down. The new plant would then provide luck throughout the year.

In Norse Mythology, the Goddess, Frīgg, the equivalent of the Anglo-Saxon Frīge, had a son who was killed by a spear poisoned with mistletoe. After seeing that her son was dead, it was Frīgg's tears that turned into the white berries that grow upon the mistletoe. Frīgg then placed these berries on her son's chest, causing him to come back to life. Frīgg then praised the mistletoe as a symbol of love and peace and promised that whoever stood beneath it would be offered a kiss and be forever protected. For centuries, it has been a Norse custom for any woman caught standing under the mistletoe to kiss the man who asked. It was considered bad luck to refuse. The Vikings believed mistletoe could bring peace. When enemies met under it, they were expected to stop fighting for the day.

In Scandinavia, Yule wreaths were made from evergreen branches, as well as holly and ivy, and were round to represent Frīgg's spinning wheel. Four candles were then placed on the wreath and were lit before being spun around to make a circle of light, a magical sign to represent the Sun and frighten away unclean spirits. Wreaths were associated with the dead and are still used in funerals today. Garlands are much like wreaths, except they aren't circular and can be wrapped around trees and people as a form of protection. The Sun Wheel is an ancient cross inside a circle and was native to countless pre-Christian cultures across Europe. In Scandinavia, during Yule, the cross is set on fire to represent the Sun's return.

Holly with its bright red berries and prickly green leaves is easily recognisable and is found everywhere during the Christmas holidays. It was an ancient Pagan custom to bring holly into the house to protect the home from fairies or at least to allow good relationships between the fairies and the human occupants. In the New Year, it was traditional for a husband to bring home the prickly-leaved holly; likewise, his wife would bring home the smooth-leaved holly. Whichever was brought into the house first dictated whether the husband or wife would rule the household for the coming year.

Because of their protective properties, there were taboos against cutting down holly trees. It was also seen as practical to leave them to grow as they formed a natural barrier against witches entering one's property. The felling of holly trees was said to bring bad luck, but it was acceptable to take boughs of holly for decoration and the coppicing of trees to provide winter fodder for livestock. John Campbell, the 9th Duke of Argyll, 1845-1914, married Princess Louise, the daughter of Queen Victoria. It is said he rerouted a road in Scotland to avoid cutting down a distinctive old holly tree.

Holly was associated with Thunor and the ancient British God of Thunder, Taranis. Holly trees were often planted near one's home because they were believed to protect the house from lightning. It is now known that the spines on the holly leaves can attract lightning, and therefore protect the tree and other nearby objects, such as people's homes. The ancient Druids of Britain and Gaul (France) believed holly leaves offered protection against evil spirits and fairies, and so they wore them in their hair.

In England, it was customary on Boxing Day, the day after Christmas Day, to bleed horses in order to relieve the horse of bad spirits. It is an old Kent custom to feed cockerels a bit extra on Christmas Eve in the hope the cockerels would have more strength to frighten away bad spirits. The custom survives to this day, but it is now the ducks who are fed.

Today, Yule Logs are made of chocolate sponge and cream, but in pre-Christian times the Yule Log was literally a log that was cut down on the first day of Yule and brought into the communal hall or home. The hearth-fire was lit using a piece of wood from the previous year's Yule Log. Lighting the fire symbolised the end of darkness and the coming of light. It was also a way to warm the dead who had crossed into the world of the living. The new log was then slowly fed into the flames during Yule. It was bad luck to let the fire go out before the end of Yule. After the Winter Solstice, the tree's ashes were spread onto the farmers' fields to assure new crops in the coming year. In Germany, the ash from the Yule Log was kept all year as luck against lightning.

The modern Christmas carol singing comes from the Anglo-Saxon custom of Wassailing, where children would visit folk's homes and sing in return for a drink from the Wassail bowl. The owner of the house would say, 'Wæs hæl', which is Old English for 'be healthy'. The singers would reply, 'drinc hæl', meaning 'drink and be healthy'. Often floating in the Wassail bowl was a piece of toasted bread. The first singer would then take out the toast and wish everyone good luck. This is where the English term 'making a toast' comes from. The drink was originally mulled apple cider.

As well as folk's homes, children also gathered by private-owned cider-producing orchards, reciting incantations and singing to the apple cider trees, in order to awaken the tree spirits. The Wassail Queen would be lifted up into the boughs of the tree where she would offer a gift of toast soaked in Wassail to the friendly tree spirit. As the singing continued, the assembled crowd would throw stones and shout, as well as bang drums, pots and pans, to drive away unclean spirits. After gunpowder was invented, it became customary to fire guns at the trees, before moving onto the next orchard. This ancient tradition is still very much thriving in parts of England where cider is still produced. In Somerset, the oldest apple tree in the orchard was believed to house a spirit, known as the Apple Tree Man. A Christmas carol from the 1800s, in Somerset, reveals an old Wassailing tradition. They would sing the following lyrics after drinking the cider until they were merry:

'Apple tree, apple tree,
we all come to wassail thee,
bear this year and next year to bloom
and to blow,
hat fulls, cap fulls, three cornered sack fills,
hip, hip, hip, hurrah,
holler biys, holler hurrah.'

Part Three
Folk Dances and Pagan Traditions

Halloween

The term 'Halloween' means Hallowed Evening. It is a Christian celebration to remember the dead, especially Christian saints and martyrs. Halloween is also known as All Hallows Eve and is celebrated on the 31st of October. The day after, on the 1st of November, is known as All Saints Day. The first mention of Halloween in England is found in Old English and was known as All Hallows. It is first recorded as All Hallows' Eve in 1556. The word 'Halloween' or 'Hallowe'en' dates to 1745. I was born and raised in England, but I have never known Halloween to be a Christian celebration. I have always believed Halloween to be a Pagan night of the dead, when the spirits cross the threshold to torment the living.

Like Christmas, Halloween has Pagan roots. The Christian church could not erase the Pagan customs that took place on the 31st of October, and so they rebranded it a Christian holiday. In pre-Christian Ireland, before there was Halloween, there was the Irish fire festival of Samhain, meaning Summer's End.

The 31st October is halfway between the Autumn Equinox and the Winter Solstice. In ancient Ireland, Samhain was a Gaelic festival marking the end of the harvest season, the end of Summer and the beginning of Winter. Samhain was celebrated in Ireland, Scotland and the Isle of Man. In Wales it was known as Calan Gaeaf. In Cornwall it was known as Kalan Gwav. In Brittany, France, it was known as Kalan Goañv. Interestingly, Brittany was named after the Britons who settled there during the 5th Century when the great Anglo-Saxon incursions began. November the 1st was the beginning of the Old Irish New Year. To the Pagan Irish, Samhain was the Night of the Dead, a time to remember one's ancestors and to protect one's family from the Aos Sí, the Irish fairy folk.

In Summer, the days are long and the nights are short. Summer is a time of great prosperity and healing, it is warm, bright, comforting and life-giving. The Sun sits high in the sky, the birds are singing in the trees, food is in abundance, children are playing and everything is bursting with life and colour. It is a time of happiness where people are at their healthiest, when newborn animals are playing in the fields and there is much joy to be had. Summer is the realm of the living. In Pagan times, the thought of displeasing the Gods and the Sun disappearing, to never return, was a terrifying thought.

In Winter, the days are short and the nights are long. In October, one only has to walk outside their home to see that the Sun has gone, the leaves and fruits have fallen from the trees and are rotting on the ground. The trees are lifeless and ominously looming overhead, waiting to snatch the unsuspecting and drag them from the realm of the living. One can feel the cold biting at their flesh, threatening to take precious life away. It is a time of darkness, decay and human death. Winter is the realm of the dead. In ancient Ireland, sacrifices were made to the Gods for protection and to entice them to bring back the Sun, and great bonfires were built to push back against the darkness of Winter.

Like the Anglo-Saxon Blótmōnaþ, cattle and livestock were ritually slaughtered for the Winter. Great fires were lit to represent the return of the Sun. In Pagan Ireland, fires were magical and were believed to have cleansing powers. Sometimes, two bonfires would be built side by side, and the people, sometimes with their livestock, would walk between them as a cleansing ritual. Once cleansed, the animal would be sacrificed to the Gods, its flesh eaten and its bones thrown onto the fires. Often black sheep were used for the sacrifice. In England today, to be called the 'black sheep of the family' means that you are the odd one out, the least favourite; the one given the short straw.

Scotland is named after the Irish Clan, the Scotti, who settled in the North of Britain in the 5th Century. Though the Irish and Scots converted to Christianity several centuries earlier than the English, many of their old Pagan customs have prevailed. In Scotland, during the night of Halloween, many Samhain customs have survived, including boys who travelled from house to house asking for wood for the bonfire. When the fire was lit, the boys took turns laying down on the ground as close to the fire as possible without getting burned and allowed the smoke to roll over him. Meanwhile, the other boys ran through the smoke and jumped over him. They also took flames from the fire back to their homes and walked in every room; the smoke acting as a protection spell. When the bonfire burnt down, the boys scattered the ashes on farmers' fields to protect them and, perhaps like their Anglo-Saxon counterparts, to assure new crops in the coming year. Some families would put out their hearth fires and relight them using flames from the village's communal bonfire, an act to bond the families of the village together. In ancient Ireland, druids would gather on Samhain Night to kindle a sacred fire. From this, every bonfire in the land was lit, and from them every home relit their hearth, which had been put-out that night.

Throughout Ireland, Scotland and the Isle of Man, Samhain was a time when games were played and many rituals were performed in order to predict the future of those gathered, especially with regard to death and marriage. Apples and hazelnuts were often used in the rituals. In Irish Mythology, apples were associated with the supernatural and immortality, while hazelnuts were associated with divine wisdom. One of the most common games was apple bobbing. Another involved hanging a small wooden rod from the ceiling at head height, with a lit candle on one end and an apple hanging from the other. The rod was spun round and everyone took turns to try to catch the apple with their teeth. Apples were peeled in one long strip, the peel was then tossed over the shoulder and its shape was said to form the first letter of the future spouse's name. Two hazelnuts were roasted near a fire; one named for the person roasting them, the other for the person they desired. If the nuts jumped away from the heat, it was a bad omen, but if the nuts roasted quietly, it foretold a good match. Items were hidden in food, such as cakes. A person's future was foretold by the item they found. Egg whites were dropped in water and the shapes foretold the number of children they would one day have. In 18th Century Scotland, Wales and Brittany, a ring of stones, one for each person in attendance, was laid around the fire. Everyone ran around the circle with a flaming torch. In the morning, the stones were examined and if any were mislaid, it was said that the person it represented would not live out the year.

Like the Anglo-Saxon Yule, Samhain was a frightening time when the realm of the living and the realm of the dead is thin and the cold seeps through the gaps, along with the spirits of the dead. Though it is common today for people to dress up as witches and devils at Halloween, neither Halloween nor Samhain had anything to do with witchcraft or Satan worship. Pagans have no belief in the Devil. There was no Frankenstein, Vampires or Werewolves. However, ghosts or spirits were very real to those celebrating Samhain. The most feared were the Aos Sí, the Irish fairies.

Aos Sí means 'people of the mounds'. They were supernatural beings that lived underground in fairy mounds and inside trees. In Irish literature, the Aos Sí are described as very beautiful or ugly and hideous. At Samhain, it was believed that the Aos Sí could cross into the world of the living and cause mayhem, even injuring and killing livestock, and so they needed to be appeased to ensure the people and their livestock survived the Winter.

Like their Anglo-Saxon, German and Scandinavian counterparts, offerings of baked goods, apples or berries, accompanied by a bowl of milk, were left outside for them; it is a custom that has survived to the present day in some parts of Ireland and Scotland. In fear of the Aos Sí, people stayed near their homes or, if forced to walk in the dark, turned their clothing inside-out or carried iron or salt to keep them away.

Like the Anglo-Saxon Yule, the souls of dead kin were believed to cross the threshold and visit their loved ones. Feasts were prepared and an extra place was set at the table for dead relatives. Candles were lit and placed on one's doorstep in order to help dead relatives find their way home in the dark. Seeing a spider on the 31st of October was believed to be a dead ancestor or friend come to visit.

Much like today, dressing up played a large part in the Samhain fire festivals and involved people going door-to-door wearing animal masks and skins, reciting verses in exchange for food. In 16th Century Scotland, and perhaps much earlier, young men dressed in white robes and went house to house with blackened faces, possibly using soot from the sacred fires. The 'ghosts' would often threaten to do mischief if they weren't welcomed. The frightening costumes were not in honour of evil spirits, but to hide from them, to blend in amongst them.

In parts of Southern Ireland, during the 19th Century, it was customary for a man to cover himself in a white sheet and carry a decorated horse skull, followed by a group of youths, blowing on cow horns and travelling from farm to farm. At each farm they sang songs in exchange for food, much like the Anglo-Saxon Wassailing, the forbearer to carol singing. If the farmer donated food he could expect good fortune in the coming year, but if he refused then he could expect great misfortune. Playing pranks at Halloween is recorded in the Scottish Highlands as far back as 1736 and was also common in Ireland, which led to Halloween being nicknamed Mischief Night.

Wearing costumes at Halloween spread to England in the 20th Century, as did the custom of playing pranks. Irish and Scottish immigrants took Halloween to the United States. In America, it is customary to dress up for Halloween in traditional costumes, as well as non-traditional costumes, such as cowboys and astronauts. I can't help but feel the non-traditional costumes are Christian in influence, to steer people away from Pagan practices. Never in my life have I seen anyone in England dress up as anything but frightening costumes. To see someone dressed as a cowboy or an astronaut or a cartoon character in England on Halloween night is unthinkable.

Punkie Night

Still surviving in some Somerset villages to this day, Punkie Night is when English children parade though the streets with Jack-o'-lanterns, known as Punkies. The Punkies are made from mangelwurzel, an orange vegetable that has been used in England for centuries in times of celebration and can be turned into an alcoholic beverage. Like the American pumpkin, the top of the mangelwurzel is cut off to form a lid, the inside flesh is scooped out and a monstrous or comical face is carved out of the rind to expose the hollow interior. To create the lantern effect, a lit candle is placed inside before the lid is closed. Surprisingly, this custom has survived on the other side of England in rural Norfolk, showing how widespread the custom must have once been. The procession is traditionally led by a Punkie King and Queen, followed by adults and children who break into song:

'It's Punkie Night tonight,
it's Punkie Night tonight,
Adam and Eve would not believe,
it's Punkie Night tonight.
Give me a candle, give me a light;
if you don't, you'll get a fright.
Give me a candle,
give me light.
If you haven't a candle,
a penny's all right.'

The tradition of walking the streets with a lit mangelwurzel comes from men of a particular village who went to a fair one night and got so drunk the women had to go out and find them with home-made lanterns.

'It is an ancient British custom to light great bonfires
(Bone-fire to clear before Winter froze the ground)
on Hallowe'en,
and carry blazing fagots about on long poles;
but in place of this, American boys
delight in the funny grinning
Jack-o'-lanterns made of huge
yellow pumpkins with a candle inside.'

Halloween Sports and Customs,
Agnes Carr Sage, 1885

The heads do not represent human sacrifice as some people suggest. The term 'Jack-o'-lantern' was originally used to describe the visual phenomenon known as ignis fatuus, foolish fire, or hobby lanterns, but are better known today in English folklore as Will-o'-the-wisp, named after the phenomenon of strange lights flickering over peat bogs. The term 'wisp' refers to a bundle of sticks or paper, sometimes used as a torch. The term 'Will' refers to the name 'William'. Its earliest known use dates to the 1660s in England. Jack-o'-lantern simply means 'Jack of the lantern', and is the Irish equivalent of the English 'Will-o'-the-wisp'. The lanterns or Punkies represent good spirits or supernatural beings and were used to ward-off evil spirits. The lanterns could also be made from turnips.

> 'In my juvenile days,
> I remember to have seen peasant boys make,
> what they called a "Hoberdy's Lantern,"
> by hollowing out a turnip,
> and cutting eyes, nose and mouth therein,
> in the true moon-like style;
> and having lighted it up by inserting the stump of a candle,
> they used to place it upon a hedge
> to frighten unwary travellers in the night.'

Folklorist, Jabez Allies, 1787-1856

Today, the Halloween activities include trick-or-treating, attending Halloween costume parties, carving pumpkins into Jack-o'-lanterns, lighting bonfires, apple bobbing, playing games and pranks, visiting haunted attractions, telling scary stories and watching horror films.

The Allendale Baal Fire Festival

Every year in Northumberland, England, hundreds of people gather to witness the Allendale Baal Fire, which takes place on the 31st December to usher in the New Year. The great fire festival is believed to have been in existence since the Early Middle Ages. Men with blackened faces dance their way between houses and businesses, all the while live music is played to the crowd. As midnight approaches, the Tar Barrel Men gather in a corner of the square. The men carry shallow barrels of tar, wood shavings and a pint of paraffin across the square, forming three columns. By 11.30 PM, the torches are lit, the barrels are ignited, and the square bursts with light. The men with their blackened faces and flaming barrels upon their shoulders go on the march, before tossing the barrels onto the fourteen-foot-high pile of fir branches and set the fire alight. As the fire burns brightly, defiant of the cold, dark night sky, the band plays Auld Lang Syne, while the crowd link hands and sing along.

Morris Dancing

Morris Dancing is a form of English folk dance with obscure origins. The dancers form a group and dress in white shirts, adorned with shimmering red and green ribbons and a matching central rosette. The white long-sleeved shirts also feature turned-up cuffs with buttons. White trousers are usually worn with attached red handkerchiefs and jingling bells with red and green ribbons around the legs. The dancers also wear straw hats decorated with white, red and green flowers and a pair of white handkerchiefs. As with many Pagan traditions, the dancers also blacken their faces. Sticks, swords and handkerchiefs are also used by the dancers, who then dance to music in front of a group of onlookers.

The earliest known mention of Morris Dancing in England dates to 1448. Also in the 15th Century, records show that Morris Dancing was associated with Sword Dancing, Guising and other dances, including Mumming Plays. The modern spelling 'Morris Dance' first appears in England during the 17th Century, but has been recorded in previous centuries as Morisk Dance, Moreys Daunce, and Morisse Daunce, which all mean Moorish Dance. The term is believed to have entered the English language from Flemish, Mooriske Danse.

The origins of Morris Dancing are debatable. Scholars have suggested that the custom comes from Spanish dancers who were inspired by the Muslim Moors who invaded Spain in the 8th Century, and Sicily in the 9th Century, hence the term 'Moorish Dance'.

Cecil Sharp, 1859-1924, was the founding father of the folk-song revival in England in the early 20th Century. He also promoted Morris Dancing and founded the English Folk Dance Society in 1911. After researching the origins of Morris Dancing, Cecil came to the conclusion that English Morris Dancing and the European Moorish Dances were too dissimilar to be connected. The 20th Century folklorist, Rodney Gallop, has argued that the name 'Moorish' was used as a description of an existing earlier tradition and not because the dancers represented Muslim Moors. Rodney Gallop points out that Spain and Portugal's Moorish Dances involve mock battles between the Christians and Moors, often to music, and involve swords and handkerchiefs. Rodney Gallop suggests that the Christian-Moorish link is actually a later interpretation of earlier Pagan mock battles between Summer and Winter. He argues that in parts of Portugal and the Basque Country, the word 'moor' used to mean 'Pagan', and that perhaps Morris Dance originally meant Pagan Dance. He notes that bells and disguised faces were a common feature of Pagan rituals.

For several centuries, landowners in England wanted to privatise the use of the communal pastures, which resulted in villages being depopulated. This is known as enclosure. The English peasants responded with a series of revolts. In October 1450, a large group of men entered the Duke of Buckingham's park at Penshurst in Kent and took away eighty two deer. These armed men had blackened faces, wore long false beards and called themselves 'servants of the Queen of the Fairies.' It is argued that Morris Dancing is to commemorate those who fought against the oppressive British regime and left the English population with no land in which to build their homes. Today, in England, the land that was taken from us is rented back to us and we are given enough garden space to hang a washing-line in.

> 'In fashionable society when I was young,
> a small boy, his face daubed with black
> and his forehead swathed in a white or yellow handkerchief,
> would make an appearance after supper.
> He wore leggings covered with little bells and performed a morris.'
>
> Thoinot Arbeau, France, 1580

Interestingly, the Christmas dancers that performed in the streets of France later gave rise to what we now call Pantomime. By the 17th Century, the English working class were taking part in Morris Dances at Whitsun, the Christian festival of Pentecost. Later, the Puritan government of Oliver Cromwell suppressed Whitsun and other festivities, including Morris Dancing. They also tried to ban Christmas, saying it should be a working day. When the crown was restored by Charles II, Morris Dancing was once again restored and Christmas was saved. Morris Dancing has a long and fascinating history. We will never know of its true origins. However, I can state that the blackening of the face has nothing to do with racism, mocking other cultures, or people of African heritage. It was a way for oppressed people to hide their identities when protesting their governments. Also, there is no doubt, the blackening of one's face is an ancient Pagan custom, a way to hide from unclean spirits.

> 'As for the Harii, they are superior in strength to the other peoples
> I have just mentioned, and they pander to their savage instincts
> by choice of trickery and time.
> They black their shields and dye their bodies black
> and choose pitch dark nights for their battles.
> The terrifying shadow of such a fiendish army inspires a mortal panic,
> for no enemy can stand so strange and devilish a sight.
> Defeat in battle always begins with the eyes.'
>
> Germania,
> Cornelius Tacitus, 9 A. D.

Molly Dancing

Molly Dancing is an old English folk dance. The dance was traditionally done by out-of-work plough boys in Midwinter, during the 19th Century; though it seems to share many of the old Anglo-Saxon Pagan customs found in other folk traditions and is similar to the court jesters of the Middle Ages.

Molly Dancing is most associated with Plough Monday, when people return to work after the Twelve Days of Christmas. The plough boys would paint their faces with black soot to disguise themselves and dress up in black clothes, complete with coloured scarves. It was originally an all-male tradition, though one of the members, the Molly, dressed up as a woman. The word 'Molly' means 'an effeminate man'. The dancers would tour the village landowners, offering to dance in exchange for money. The landowners who refused to pay would be punished in various ways, similar to Halloween trick-or-treating. The dancers would return to the landowners seeking employment, hence the reason for blackening their faces, to disguise themselves. In East Anglia, the Mollies were known as Kitwitches, meaning buffoons, but were originally called Shitwitches.

In Manchester, England, Molly Dancing was once quite popular and was associated with the May Day celebrations, where boys and girls dressed as Mollies and journeyed from house to house, asking for small amounts of money. Sadly, the tradition died out in the 1950s, possibly due to immigration from India and the Caribbean. Also, the post-war slum clearance programmes resulted in the widespread demolition of housing and the break-up of communities throughout Manchester. Today, Molly Dancers can be seen all around the country at various folk dances and lives on in the spirit of Halloween.

Darkie Day

Darkie Day or Mummer's Day is a Pagan, Midwinter celebration that occurs every year on Boxing Day and New Year's Day in Padstow, Cornwall, England. It is an ancient custom where the people of Cornwall disguise themselves by painting their faces black and wear dark clothing, representing the Winter Solstice. Darkie Day was originally called Darking Day, due to the dark Winter nights and the wearing of masks or face paint. The Montol Festival in Penzance, Cornwall, is a similar Winter Solstice celebration, during which people guise dance with their faces and skin painted black.

The Abbots Bromley Horn Dance

The Abbots Bromley Horn Dance is an English folk dance dating back to pre-Christian times and involves dancers wearing reindeer horns. Reindeer were native to Britain until going extinct thousands of years ago. The dance takes place each year in Abbots Bromley, a village in Staffordshire, England. The modern version of the dance involves reindeer antlers, a Hobby Horse, Maid Marian and a Fool. The use of antlers have Pagan origins and represent the forest, fertility and masculinity.

Since 1660, the dance has taken place on Wakes Monday, the day following Wakes Sunday, which is the first Sunday after the 4th September. Violet Alford, a student of folklore and folk dance, wrote in 1940 that the dance had previously taken place on the Twelfth Day of Christmas, during the first week of January. The dance has also been performed on Christmas Day and New Year's Day. There are twelve dancers in total, six of which carry the horns and are accompanied by a musician playing the accordion. A violin was used in older times, and maybe a lyre before that, like the one found at the famous Sutton Hoo burial site in East Anglia. Maid Marian is played by a man in drag. There is also a Hobby Horse, a Fool or Jester, a young boy with a bow and arrow, representing Robin Hood, and another boy with a triangle. Traditionally, the dancers were all male, though in recent years girls have been taking part.

Whittlesea Straw Bear Festival

The Festival of the Straw Bear or Strawbower is an English Pagan custom found in a small area of Fenland, on the borders of Huntingdonshire and Cambridgeshire. On Plough Tuesday, the day after Plough Monday, the first Monday after the Twelfth Night of Christmas, a man or boy transforms into a bear by dressing in a costume made entirely of straw. The costume weighs approximately 70lbs. The bear dances around the streets with its 'keeper', alongside musicians, a plough and a plough team, and followed by Morris Dancers, Molly Dancers, Longsword Dancers and Clog Dancers. The 'keeper' leads the bear from house to house, where he dances in exchange for money, food or beer.

In the evening, in public houses, there are poetry readings followed by a combination of folk music, folk dancing, singing and story telling. Sometimes, a Hobby Horse also takes part. After the event, the bear costume is ritually burned. The custom died out by the early 20th Century, possibly due to police regarding it as begging, but it was revived by the Whittlesea Society in 1980. Today, the festival is spread over two days, Saturday and Sunday.

Hoodening

Hoodening, also spelled Hodening and Oodening, is an ancient Pagan custom found in Kent, England and involves folks carrying the heads of sacrificed horses in a ritual dance. In more recent times, Hoodening is performed on Christmas Eve by groups of farm labourers. A horse's head made of wood, with a hinged jaw that can be moved by a string, is attached to a four-foot-long wooden pole and paraded through the village like a real horse, accompanied by farmers and several musicians. The group carry the horse's head to local houses and shops, where they sing in return for money or food. Once inside, the horse prances and gnashes its jaw, while the jockey attempts to mount it, and the Molly, (a man dressed as an old woman and often depicted with a blackened face), sweeps the floor with his broom whilst chasing away any girls present, until being paid off with money or food. Once payment is received, they move on to the next house.

'I remember as a child being taken out on Christmas Eve
to the High Street in Deal,
where the shops would be open very late,
and it was the only time Deal children were allowed out in the evening;
parents were very strict.
As we would be looking at the lighted shops,
and listening to the people selling their wares,
a horrible growl, and a long horse's face would appear,
resting on our shoulder, and when one looked round,
there would be a long row of teeth snapping at us with its wooden jaws.
It was frightening for a child.
Usually, there would be a man leading the horse with a rope,
and another covered over with sacks or blankets as the horse.'

Naomi Wiffen of Edenbridge, writing in the early 1980s

Academics agree, Hoodening is Pagan in origins, but the name does not relate to Wōden or Odin, as one might suspect, but comes from the term 'hooded', a reference to the sackcloth worn by the individual carrying the horse. It is possible the custom is linked to an ancient horse sacrifice to Wōden. Also, perhaps more likely, Hoodening is to commemorate the arrival of the Jutes, in the year 449, led by Hengist and Horsa (the stallion and the horse). I believe it is likely that Hengist and Horsa arrived in Kent from Horsens (Land of the Horse), Jutland, and brought with them the emblem of a white horse against a red background. To this day, both Horsens and Kent bear the flag of a white horse against a red background. I believe I am the first person to make this connection.

The earliest known written account of Hoodening was published in a May 1807 edition of European Magazine. The article was based on an old letter, written by an anonymous individual who was describing their encounter with the Hoodeners on a visit to the Kentish coastal town of Ramsgate, in Thanet. The letter reads:

'I found they begin the festivities of Christmas by a curious procession: a party of young people procure the head of a dead horse, which is affixed to a pole about four-feet in length; a string is affixed to the lower jaw; a horse-cloth is also attached to the whole, under which one of the parts gets, and by frequently pulling the string, keeps up a loud snapping noise, and is accompanied by the rest of the party, grotesquely habited, with hand-bells; they thus proceed from house to house, ringing their bells, and singing carols and songs. They are commonly gratified with beer and cake, or perhaps with money. This is called, provincially, a Hodening.'

In December 1889, a letter written by a resident of St. Lawrence named Charles J. H. Saunders appeared in The Bromley Record. Mr Saunders stated that he had spoken with many elderly residents of Thanet about Hoodening and they had informed him that the custom had been discontinued for around fifty years, after a woman in Broadstairs was so scared by the hooden horse she died. Although this practice had vanished by the time of World War One, it has since made a comeback and is now incorporated into various Kentish plays, such as Mumming and Morris Dancing, which take place at different times of the year.

Hobby Horse

The Hobby Horse is an old Pagan relic, similar to Hoodening, and is associated with the May Day celebrations, Mumming and Morris Dancing. The horses are made from a circular framework, tightly covered with shiny black material, carried on the shoulders of a dancer whose face is hidden by a grotesque mask attached to a tall, pointed hat. A skirt hangs down from the horse and covers the rider's knees. At the front of the body there is a wooden horse head with snapping jaws, attached to a long, straight neck, with a long mane. At the back of the horse there is a small tail made of horsehair.

It is traditional for two or more horses to be surrounded by bands of loyal supporters, while a man waves a padded club and dances in front of the horses. The procession then makes its way through the streets, accompanied by a lively band of accordions and drummers playing a traditional May Song. The horses sometimes capture young women beneath the skirt of the Hobby Horse. Later, the women emerge from the horse smeared in black. The horses' visits were to bring good luck. The music and drums, I believe, was to frighten away bad spirits.

Mumming and Guising

Mumming, or Momerie as it is sometimes called, is an ancient Pagan custom that still survives to this day in England and is often performed at Christmas, Easter and Plough Monday. It is sometimes called Guising. It is a traditional play where men dress up in costumes and perform in certain villages across England. The play involves a champion who is killed in a fight, but is then brought back to life by a doctor. In England, since the late 16th Century, the champion has often been Saint George who does battle with a dragon, but is later killed. He is then brought back to life and slays the dragon.

The original Pagan play has been lost, but may have been Siegfried overcoming the ferocious dragon, Fafnir. It is likely that Siegfried represented the Sun, but is killed by the dragon, representing Winter, only for Siegfried to be resurrected, representing the return of the Sun. The story of Siegfried is German, but Siegfried was known to the English people and can be found in the Bēowulf poem, which pre-dates the German Nibelungenlied by at least two hundred years.

Mumming was a popular amusement across Europe between the 13th and 16th Centuries and involved bands of masked men parading through the streets during Winter festivals and entering houses to dance or play dice in complete silence. Its origins are so old they cannot be traced. The word 'mumming' may come from the German word mumme, meaning mask, or masker, or the Greek mommo, meaning frightening mask. Mumming and Guising were plays that were passed on from father to son, until the First World War, where many sons and fathers were killed on the battlefield. It has since been revived.

May Day

May Day is an ancient Pagan custom celebrated in England and around the world. The celebrations include crowning a May Queen and dancing around the Maypole. Historically, Morris Dancing has been associated with the May Day celebrations. The celebrations date back to the Pagan Anglo-Saxon customs held during þrimilcimōnaþ, the Month of Three Milkings. May Day was abolished by Puritan parliaments, but was reinstated with the restoration of Charles II in 1660.

May Day is a celebration where large gatherings raise garlands and celebrate the springtime fertility of the soil, livestock and people. Seeding the fields has been completed and May Day is the farmers' well-earned day off work. The most important part of the tradition is the tall wooden pole called a Maypole, where young girls traditionally dance around the pole in a circle, with long ribbons. The pole was often made from a birch tree, which has a long history and is associated with Paganism. The pole is an ancient custom used primarily in Germanic countries, such as Germany and England and the neighbouring areas that they have influenced, such as Scotland, Wales and North America. The Maypole is likely to be an ancient remnant of the Germanic worship of sacred trees, such as Thunor's Oak, the Irminsul and tree at Uppsala.

On May Day, in Oxford, England, it is an old tradition for people to gather below the Great Tower of Magdalen College to listen to the college choir sing traditional madrigals. Later, the people jump off Magdalen Bridge into the River Cherwell. The bridge is now closed on May Day due to health and safety.

On May Day, the people of Cornwall hold their annual Hobby Horse festivities, which is one of the oldest fertility rites in England. The participants dance through the streets, accompanied by accordion players and followers, who sing a traditional May Day song. The whole town is decorated with Springtime greenery and every year thousands of onlookers attend. In recent decades, the May Day celebrations have seen a huge rise in popularity and are celebrated all across the UK and often include Morris Dancers, complete with blackened faces, much like their Pagan forefathers.

Jack in the Green

In England, during the 16th and 17th Centuries, people made garlands of flowers and leaves for the May Day celebrations. Over time, the garlands became more elaborate, to the point that men wore large, foliage-covered, garland-like frameworks, covering their entire body, from head to foot. This became known as Jack in the Green. For unknown reasons, the figure of Jack in the Green became associated with chimney sweeps. By the turn of the 20th Century, the custom had started to wane as a result of Victorian disapproval. The Lord and Lady of the May, with their practical jokes, were replaced by the May Queen, while the noisy, drunken Jack in the Green vanished altogether from the parades. Though, in recent times, Jack in the Green has been revived in many English counties and vary slightly from town to town.

In Ilfracombe, North Devon, the Jack in the Green procession has been celebrated since 2000. The procession is supported by local schoolchildren dancing around the Maypole on the sea front, and by Morris Dancers. In Whitstable, Kent, Jack is accompanied by two attendants, representing Robin Hood and Maid Marian. In Hastings, Sussex, Jack is accompanied by attendants, known as Bogies, who are completely disguised in green rags, vegetation and face paint. The attendants play music, dance and sing as they guide Jack through the streets to celebrate the coming of Summer. The Hastings celebrations are one of the biggest in the country.

In Deptford, south-east London, the Fowler's Troop and Blackheath Morris have been parading the tallest and heaviest modern Jack for decades. At the end of May, a Jack is an essential part of the Pagan Pride parade in Holborn. In Bristol, Jack in the Green appears on the first Saturday in May and leads a procession through the streets of Bristol, ending the day on Horfield Common, where he is 'killed' and ripped apart by onlookers to release the spirit of Summer. In Carshalton, London, a harvest celebration takes place in September. A Jack made of straw is ritually stripped in the evening so those present can take a keepsake, before the straw figure is burnt in a brazier.

Similar characters to the English Jack in the Green are found in parts of Europe and Russia. Some include mock sacrifice, where the leafy framework is thrown or ducked into a pond or river, sometimes with the person still inside it. These festivities are associated with Easter Monday, Saint George's Day, May Day, and Whitsuntide. Sometimes, the disguise is straw rather than leaves, similar to the straw bears of German Carnival and the English Whittlesea Straw Bear Festival.

The Celebration of Golowan

The celebration of Golowan is an ancient Pagan Midsummer festival, celebrated in Cornwall, England. The terms 'Golowan' and 'Goluan' mean 'Midsummer' in the Cornish language. Today, the celebrations attract tens of thousands of people and include the lighting of bonfires, fireworks and the performance of rituals.

'In Cornwall, the festival fires, called bonfires,
are kindled on the Eve of St. John the Baptist and St. Peter's Day;
and Midsummer is thence, in the Cornish tongue, called 'Goluan',
which signifies both light and rejoicing.
At these fires the Cornish attend with lit torches,
tarred and pitched at the end,
and make their perambulations round their fires,
and go from village to village carrying their torches before them;
and this is certainly the remains of the Druid superstition,
for 'faces praeferre,' to carry lighted torches,
was reckoned a kind of Gentilism,
and as such particularly prohibited by the Gallick Councils:
they were in the eye of the law 'accensores facularum,'
and thought to sacrifice to the devil, and to deserve capital punishment.'

Antiquities of Cornwall,
Dr William Borlase, 1754

As the fires died down, the youngsters in the town would take part in the ancient serpent dance and jump through the dying embers of the flames. Two descriptions from the Victorian Period survive:

'In Penzance, and in nearly all the parishes of West Penwith,
immediately after nightfall
on the eves of St John and St Peter, the 23rd and 28th of June,
lines of tar-barrels, occasionally broken by bonfires,
were simultaneously lighted in all the streets,
whilst, at the same time, bonfires were kindled on all the cairns
and hills around Mounts Bay,
throwing the outlines in bold relief against the sky.'

'Then the villagers, linked in circles hand-in-hand,
danced round them to preserve themselves against witchcraft,
and when they burnt low, one person here and there
detached himself from the rest and leaped through the flames
to insure himself from some special evil.
The old people counted these fires and drew a presage from them.'

The Hobby Horse also takes part in the celebrations.

'Another essential character is Old Penglaze
who has a blackened face and a staff in his hand,
and a person girded round with a horse's hide,
to serve as his horse.
The master then goes up to the delinquent and,
taking up his foot, says:
"Here is my seal, where is old Penglaze's seal?"
Old Penglaze then comes in on his horse
which winces and capers about grotesquely.
The shoe of the colt is taken off and Penglaze gives him
one or two hard blows on the sole of the foot,
after which he rides off again;
his horse capering more than ever before
and sometimes throwing the old gentleman off.'

Author William Sandys,
1792-1874

Part Four
Folklore

The Wild Hunt

The modern image of Santa Claus or Father Christmas riding the dark night sky is based on Wōden and the Wild Hunt. The Wild Hunt is a group of supernatural huntsmen, Wolf-Coats, Bear-Shirts (berserkers) and other noble warriors, who have died an honourable death, weapon in hand, dripping with the blood of their enemy. The huntsmen wear the coats of wolves or bears and cover their exposed flesh with black soot. They travel the Winter sky on a chariot, pulled along by black horses, black goats and black hounds, in mad pursuit of trolls and giants.

In 1127, sixty-one-years after the Norman Conquest, English monks had a new unpleasant French abbot imposed on them, Abbot Henry of Poitou. In the Peterborough Chronicle, written in Old English, the monks wrote about their new abbot, which included a description of the Wild Hunt:

'Everything he could take, he took over seas.
He did nothing for the monastery's welfare
and left nothing untouched.
Let no one be surprised at the truth of what we are about to relate,
for it was general knowledge throughout
the whole country that immediately after his arrival,
it was Sunday 6th February,
many men saw and heard a great number of huntsmen hunting.
The huntsmen were black, huge and hideous,
and rode on black horses and on black he-goats,
and their hounds were jet black, with eyes like saucers, and horrible.
This was seen in the very deer park of the town of Peterborough,
and in all the woods that stretch from that same town to Stamford.
In the night, the monks heard them sounding and winding their horns.
Reliable witnesses were said to have given the number
of huntsmen as twenty or thirty.
This was seen from the time of his (the abbot's) arrival,
all through Lent and ending at Easter.
Such was his entrance; of his exit we cannot say.'

In January 1091, the Anglo-Norman chronicler, Orderic Vitalis, reported a similar sight in Normandy:

'Another class of spectres will prove more fruitful for our investigation: they, like the ignis fatuus (Will-o'-the-wisp), include unchristened babes, but instead of straggling singly on the earth as fires, they sweep through forest and air in whole companies with a horrible din. This is the widely spread legend of the furious host, the furious hunt, which is of high antiquity, and interweaves itself, now with gods, and now with heroes. Look where you will, it betrays its connection with heathenism.'

In Germany, during the Middle Ages, the Wild Hunt was known as Wuotanes her, meaning Wōden's army. A Christian charm dating from the 14th Century, in Germany, reads:

'May the supreme Numen divinium, may the holy sanctus spiritus, may the sacred sanctus dominus, again protect me this night from the evil creatures that roam the darkness and I sign myself against the black ones and the white ones whom people call the Good ones and who leave from Brockelsberg, against the bilwizze, against the moon eaters, against those who walk outside the paths, against the hedge riders, against the resounding invantations, against all the evil spirits! Glozan and Lodevan, Trutan and Wodan, Wōden's Army (the Wild Hunt) and all its members who bear wheels and rags, dead broken on the wheel and hung, go far from me.'

In Denmark and Germany, the Twelfth Day of Christmas had strict rules. Spinning and baking, the primary jobs for women, were forbidden. Distaffs which the wool or flax was wound were ceremonially bound with flowers to prevent them from being used and to prevent Wōden and his Wild Huntsmen from getting tangled. Baking was also banned on the Twelfth Day of Christmas because it was considered an open invitation to the Wild Huntsmen. Doors and windows were kept shut to avoid the Huntsmen creeping into people's homes and taking up residence.

'The passage of the Wild Hunt,
which, in the traditions after the Middle Ages,
was closely connected to food and drink,
is perfectly logical to us, once we grasp the role played by the dead.
They presided over the fertility of the soil and the fruitfulness of livestock. Thus it was necessary to appease them if they were regarded as neutral or well-intentioned or to drive them away and send them fleeing if they were seen as wicked.
In one way or another, the Wild Hunt fell into the vast complex of ancestor worship, the cult of the dead, who are the go-betweens between men and the Gods.'

Phantom Armies of the Night:
The Wild Hunt and the Ghostly Processions of the Undead
Claude Lecouteux

Krampus

Krampus is not associated with the Anglo-Saxons and there is no record of him found in Britain; however, he is associated with Christmas and is of Pagan origins, and so worthy of a mention.

The Feast of Saint Nicholas, the Saint of Children, is celebrated in many European countries on the 6th December. The day before is known in Austria as Krampusnacht or Krampus Night, a time when Krampus walks the streets and visits people's homes to punish naughty children. Krampus is described as half demon, half goat and has black or brown fur and the cloven hooves and horns of a goat, similar to the Christian Devil. He also has a long pointed tongue which lolls out. He is often depicted carrying chains which he thrashes for dramatic effect. The chains are sometimes accompanied with bells. He also carries bundles of birch branches called ruten, which is significant in many Pagan cultures. In contrast to Saint Nicholas rewarding good children with nice presents, Krampus visits the homes of naughty children and beats them with birch bundles, before leaving them the gift of coal.

'There seems to be little doubt as to his true identity for, in no other form is the full regalia of the Horned God of the Witches so well preserved.
The birch - apart from its phallic significance -
may have a connection with the initiation rites of certain witch-covens;
rites which entailed binding and scourging as a form of mock-death.
The chains could have been introduced
in a Christian attempt to "bind the Devil",
but again they could be a remnant of Pagan initiation rites.'

The Krampus in Styria, Maurice Bruce, 1958

In traditional parades, known as the Krampuslauf, meaning Krampus run, young men dress as Krampus and parade through the streets. Writing in 1975 about his time in Irdning, a small town in Styria, Austria, anthropologist John J. Honigmann wrote:

> 'The Saint Nicholas festival we are describing incorporates cultural elements widely distributed in Europe; in some cases going back to pre-Christian times. Nicholas himself became popular in Germany around the eleventh century. The feast dedicated to this patron of children is only one winter occasion in which children are the objects of special attention; others being Martinmas, the Feast of the Holy Innocents, and New Year's Day.
> Masked devils acting boisterously and making nuisances of themselves are known in Germany since at least the sixteenth century while animal masked devils combining dreadful-comic antics appeared in Medieval church plays.
> A large literature, much of it by European folklorists, bears on these subjects. Austrians in the community we studied are quite aware of "heathen" elements being blended with Christian elements in the Saint Nicholas customs and in other traditional winter ceremonies.
> They believe Krampus derives from a Pagan supernatural who was assimilated to the Christian devil. The Krampus figures persisted, and by the 17th Century, Krampus had been incorporated into Christian winter celebrations by pairing Krampus with St Nicholas.'

Krampus was often depicted wearing a sack or a basket strapped to his back. The sack was used to cart off naughty children to be drowned, eaten, or taken to Hell.

In the Netherlands, the 5th December is known as Sinterklaasavond, the eve of Saint Nicholas; a time when Black Peter, the companion of Saint Nicholas, walks the streets, visits schools, and scatters sweets on the ground for well-behaved children. He also carries a whip and strikes at naughty children who reach down to pick up the sweats. Traditionally, Black Peter is said to be black because he is a Muslim Moor from Spain. Those portraying Black Peter typically blacken their face and wear colourful Renaissance attire, as well as curly wigs, red lipstick and earrings.

At first sight, Krampus' goat-like, devilish appearance seems terrifying, but our Pagan ancestors may not have been so frightened. After all, goats were sacred to Thunor and many Pagans would have been in close contact with them; they would have drank their milk, ate their cheese and may have had goats as pets. Krampus may have once had more in common with Pan, the Greek God of the wild, shepherds and flocks, music, fertility and companion of the nymphs, than the Christian Devil. Pan had the hindquarters, legs and horns of a goat, similar to the Greek faun. There is no doubt amongst scholars that Satan's modern image comes from the Middle Ages and was based on Pan. It is possible that Christians gave Krampus a similar fate to Pan and demonised him, quite literally and unjustly.

Based upon the evidence, I don't believe Krampus was a malevolent figure, but was a force for good. Krampus appears during December, a time when the veil between the living and the dead is thin and spirits cross the threshold to haunt the living. I believe the naughty children were thought to be possessed by bad spirits that had crossed into the world of the living. Krampus beat the children with ruten, not as a punishment, but to drive away the bad spirits. After all, Krampus used bundles of birch brambles to beat the children with, and birch was used in countless Pagan cultures to drive away bad spirits.

> 'The birch has always been associated with the spirits of the dead and with those that mourn, for, in sympathy with the sorrowing, weeps the birch of silverbark with long dishevelled hair.'
>
> Trees and How They Grow,
> G Clarke Nuttal, 1913

It was once common to make babies' cots from birch wood because of their protective qualities and their ability to drive away unclean spirits. Bundles of birch were used to make brooms. To clean one's dusty floor with a broom made from birch sticks removed more than dust from the home. It also helped to remove bad spirits. It is said that witches' brooms were also made from birch sticks. I believe the beating of children with birch sticks may have been a kind of exorcism rather than a punishment. Also, the bells that Krampus carries is an old Pagan tradition to frighten away bad spirits, a custom that survives to this day - we decorate our Christmas Trees with them.

Krampus may have once been a God, a healer of children, or perhaps a spirit of some-kind; a force for good. Christian writers, understandably so, may have misunderstood him and condemned him as the punisher of children. On a personal note, I believe Krampus was simply a Pagan priest who dressed in a bearskin or wolfskin and wore the mask and horns of a goat, which was once a common Yule costume. He would have visited people's homes and offered to exercise the bad spirits from the house. It would have also been a great way to make sure the kids behaved. After all, like Halloween or Samhain, Yule was a time for mischief. The coal that Krampus would leave behind as a gift may seem like a punishment for naughty children, but in times past a piece of coal would have been a good gift, for it helped to feed the fire spirits and warm one's house, both for the living and the return of dead relatives. Fires also have cleansing properties and help to repel bad spirits. Fires are also lit in defiance of the cold, dark Winter and are a symbol of the Sun's return after Winter. Of course, I could be wrong, it's just a theory.

Belsnickel

Belsnickel is a fur-clad, mask wearing Christmas gift-bringing figure found in the folklore of south-western Germany. He is a servant of Saint Nicholas, but unlike other servants, Belsnickel doesn't accompany Saint Nicholas, but instead visits alone. He is described as ragged and dishevelled, wears torn, tattered and dirty clothes, has a long Krampus-like tongue and carries a bundle of birch brambles in his hand that he beats naughty children with. He also has pockets full of cakes, sweats and nuts for good children. In Lower Austria, Belsnickel is sometimes followed by Krampus, covered with bells and dragging chains.

'We didn't hear of Santa Claus.
Instead, the tradition called for a visit
by a different character altogether.
He was known as Kriskinkle, Beltznickle
and sometimes as the Christmas woman.
Children then not only saw the mysterious person,
but felt him or rather his stripes upon their backs with his switch.
The annual visitor would make his appearance some hours after dark,
thoroughly disguised, especially the face,
which would sometimes be covered with a hideously ugly phiz,
generally wore a female garb,
hence the name Christmas woman.
Sometimes it would be a veritable woman
but with masculine force and action.
He or she would be equipped with an ample sack
about the shoulders filled with cakes, nuts and fruits,
and a long hazel switch which was supposed
to have some kind of a charm in it as well as a sting.
One would scatter the goodies upon the floor,
and then the scramble would begin by the delighted children,
and the other hand would ply the switch upon the backs of the excited
youngsters who would not show a wince,
but had it been parental discipline
there would have been screams to reach a long distance.'

Jacob Brown, writing in the 19th Century

Holda

The name Holda comes from the German words for gracious, friendly, sympathetic, and grateful. In German folklore, Holda was the protectress of agriculture and women's crafts and was associated with Yule. She is described as a shining, youthful maiden, wearing clothes as white as snow, but she could also appear as an old snaggle-toothed, crooked-nosed woman. She is often depicted wearing a crown with candles or carrying a lantern. It is likely that her horrible appearance was to frighten away bad spirits during Yule, when the veil between the living and the dead was thin.

Though Holda appears to be unmarried and has no children of her own, she was the protectress of children, a kind spirit who would rock a child's cradle when its nurse fell asleep. She also owns a sacred pool, through which the souls of newborn children enter the world. Her festival was during Midwinter, when people retreated indoors to escape the cold and when the dead are able to walk amongst the living. Holda leads a procession of the dead and was associated with the Wild Hunt. I believe her feast day was the night before the Winter Solstice, as this was the night of the Wild Hunt and the Anglo-Saxon Mother's Night. When it snows, it was believed Holda was shaking out her feather pillows. Also, fog was believed to be smoke from her fire, and thunder was when she reeled her flax.

Like the Anglo-Saxon Goddess, Frīge, Holda uses a wheel to spin and weave and is connected to the spirit world. It is said when she spins, she makes the clouds. Because of this, Holda has become associated with witchcraft in Catholic German folklore. During the Middle Ages, she was thought to ride with witches on distaffs, which closely resembles witches brooms. In the beginning of the 11th Century, Holda was believed to be the leader of women and female nocturnal spirits. These women were said to leave their houses in spirit only, leaving the house through closed doors in the dead of night, leaving their sleeping husbands behind. They would travel vast distances through the sky, to great feasts, or to great battles amongst the clouds. It is very likely these battles were connected with Wōden and the Wild Hunt.

The 9th Century Canon Episcopi talks about women who claim to have ridden with a crowd of demons. Burchard's later recension of the same text expands on this in a section entitled De arte magica:

'Have you believed there is some female,
whom the stupid vulgar call Holda or, in some manuscripts, strigam
Holdam, the witch Holda, who is able to do a certain thing,
such that those deceived by the devil affirm themselves by necessity and
by command to be required to do, that is, with a crowd of demons
transformed into the likeness of women, on fixed nights to be required to
ride upon certain beasts, and to themselves be numbered in their
company? If you have performed participation in this
unbelief, you are required to do penance for one year
on designated fast-days.'

Holda features in some pre-Christian Alpine traditions that have survived into modern times. During the Christmas period in the Alpine regions of Germany, Austria and Northern Switzerland, wild masked processions are still held in certain towns, impersonating Holda, Perchta, and the Wild Hunt. Holda is remembered today in German fairy tales and is known as Frau Holle.

Perchta

Perchta is a German Goddess whose name means Bright One. She is also known as Berchta, which gives us the female name, Bertha. Like Holda, Perchta is associated with spinning and the Twelve Days of Christmas. She also has two forms and can appear as beautiful and as white as snow, or as elderly and haggered. Like Holda, it is likely that her horrible appearance was to frighten away bad spirits during Yule.

Perchta is said to roam the countryside at Midwinter and enter people's homes during the Twelve Nights of Christmas. Like Santa, she would know whether the children had behaved and worked hard all year. If they had been good, she would leave them a small silver coin. If they had been naughty, she would slit their bellies open, remove their stomach and guts and stuff them with straw and pebbles. She was particularly interested to see that young girls had spun the whole of their allotted portion of flax or wool during the year. The concept of good Pagan children being rewarded in December, and naughty children being punished, survives to this day with Santa's naughty list that he checks twice, to find out who is naughty or nice.

It was customary to offer Perchta food and drink in exchange for wealth, which was later condemned in Bavaria during the 15th Century. On Perchta's feast day, it was traditional to eat a meal of fish and gruel, but if you would dare eat anything else, then she would find you and split your belly open and stuff you with straw and pebbles.

Wolf-Coats, Werewolves and Dog-Headed People

The term 'werewolf' conjures up images of eyebrows that join in the middle and men morphing into larger-than-life wolves and howling at the Moon, before running through the forest, seeking victims to devour, only to wake up in the morning, naked, wondering what had happened. This image comes to us from the Middle Ages, through Christian lenses. Christian writers may have had some knowledge on the wolf cult of Wōden and its various practices, but did not understand them, or they simply wished to demonise them and frighten their readers and listeners. The word 'werewolf' comes from the Old English 'werwulf', meaning man-wolf. In Pagan times, the term werewolf had no negative connotations to it; in fact, it was an honour to join the King's elite warriors, the Wolf-Coats. In Anglo-Saxon times, to see a wolf before battle was considered a good omen.

In old Anglo-Saxon society, and across the Germanic world, the sons and daughters of noble warriors would leave their parents at the age of seven. They were to enter the forest and live feral, as outlaws (wulfeshéafodes), as an Army of the Dead, in order to hunt and kill wolves. The Old English term 'wulfeshéafod' means 'wolf head', and was someone who could be killed on sight. The Norse word 'Úlfhéðnar' means 'men clad in wolf skins', singular 'Úlfheðinn', and is mentioned in the Vatnsdæla Saga, Haraldskvæði and the Völsunga Saga. The Úlfhéðnar were said to wear the pelt of a wolf when they entered battle. The earliest surviving reference to the term 'berserker' is in Haraldskvæði, a poem composed by Thórbiörn Hornklofi in the late 9th Century, in honour of King Harald Fairhair:

'I'll ask of the berserks, you tasters of blood,
those intrepid heroes, how are they treated, those who wade out into battle? Wolf-skinned they are called. In battle they bear bloody shields.
Red with blood are their spears when they come to fight.
They form a closed group. The prince in his wisdom puts trust in such men who hack through enemy shields.'

The Icelandic historian and poet, Snorri Sturluson, wrote the following description of berserkers in the Ynglinga Saga:

'His (Odin's) men rushed forwards without armour,
were as mad as dogs or wolves,
bit their shields, and were strong as bears or wild oxen,
and killed people at a blow,
but neither fire nor iron told upon them.
This was called going berserk.'

The oldest evidence for Wolf-Coats were found in Russia and date back four thousand years. Excavations at Krasnosamarskoe found thousands of dog bones, eighteen wolf bones and six bones that came from either dogs or wolves. Many of the dog bones were charcoaled and were found to have human teeth marks on them, proving they had been cooked and eaten. Many of the dogs' skulls were chopped into small pieces in a ritualistic and skillful manner. Cattle and sheep bones were also found at the site and show signs of butchery and cooking, but their skulls had not been chopped up. Microscopic analyses of the teeth indicated that most of the dogs had been killed during the Winter, which coincides with the Anglo-Saxon practice of young Wolf-Coats living wild during the Winter.

Young boys being tossed into the wild and left to fend for themselves, in order to hunt and kill wolves, to prove their worth, may be the explanation behind the Cynocephali, the infamous dog-headed people. Throughout history there have been many reports of races of jackal-headed or dog-headed people. In Egyptian Mythology, there were dog-headed Gods, such as Wepwawet, Anubis, Horus, and his son, Duamutef. The Greek traveller and historian, Megasthenes, 350-290 BC, knew about dog-headed people in India, who lived in the mountains, communicated through barking, wore the skins of wild animals and lived by hunting. In the 2nd Century, a Greek historian wrote how the Cynocephali caught their food and roasted it in the Sun; how they kept sheep, but couldn't speak with the tongue of man. They understood the Indian language and drank milk from their animals. He also talks about a similar race of people on the road to Ethiopia, who were black of skin. They couldn't speak but uttered a shrill squeal. Their bodies were covered in hair and they had the head and teeth of a dog.

In the 5th Century, a Greek physician named Ctesias also wrote about the Cynocephali in India. In the mountains, he saw men with heads of dogs who didn't talk but barked; they had larger teeth than dogs, and claws like animals. They were known to live on raw meat and fruit and hunted with bows and arrows. They traded with the local Indians and sent tributes to the King of India. They lived in caves, wore tanned skins, and all had a tail like a dog's, only longer.

The famous adventurer, Marco Polo, wrote about dog-headed barbarians that lived and grew spices on the Andaman Islands in Asia. He said they were cruel and were just like big mastiff dogs. In China, a Buddhist missionary named Hui-Sheng wrote about dog-headed men on an island to the east of Fusang.

> 'They pretend that they have in their camps Cynocephali,
> that is, men with dogs' heads.
> They spread the rumour among the enemy that these men
> wage war obstinately, drink human blood
> and quaff their own gore if they cannot reach the foe.'
>
> Historia gentis Langobardorum
> (History of the Long-beards),
> Paul the Deacon, 720-799 A. D.

The Nowell Codex, the same manuscript that contains the Anglo-Saxon epic, Bēowulf, also contains references to the dog-headed people. In the manuscript, known as The Wonders of the East, they are called Healfhundingas, meaning half-dogs.

> 'In January, every eight years,
> the inhabitants of the Lejre region (Hleidargard)
> - in other words, Roskilde, in Sjaelland (Zealand), Denmark,
> sacrifice dogs and cocks to the Gods.'
>
> German chronicler, Thietmar of Merseburg, 975-1018

Trajan's Column, in Rome, completed in 113 A. D., depicts Germanic warriors fighting on behalf of Rome. They had big beards and were dressed in wolf pelts that covered their head and shoulders, and down their backs, leaving their arms free.

The Winnili were a Germanic Clan whose name meant howlers. According to legend, Wōden would later change their name to the Lombards, meaning Long-beards.

Across the Norse and Germanic world, evidence of the ancient wolf cult of Wōden/Odin has been found in many graves. The most famous is, of course, the Sutton Hoo Treasure. Sutton Hoo, in Suffolk, East Anglia was the site of two 6th and 7th Century Anglo-Saxon burial mounds. One of the mounds contained an undisturbed ship-burial similar to the Viking longship, and included a wealth of Anglo-Saxon artefacts, including the world famous Sutton Hoo Helmet, now housed in the British Museum in London. Amongst the artefacts is the Sutton Hoo purse lid which is considered to be one of the most remarkable creations of the Early Middle Ages. At seven-and-a-half-inches-long, the lid is decorated with gold and garnet cloisonné enamel, and was without a doubt a symbol of great wealth and status. Interestingly, the purse lid features two separate warriors, each in combat against two wolves, which may be evidence of England's forgotten Wolf-Coat culture.

Though no body was ever found at the site, it is believed that the treasures belonged to King Rædwald of East Anglia, who reigned between 599 and 624. King Rædwald belonged to the famous Wuffing dynasty, an English royal clan named after wolves. As well as King of East Anglia, Rædwald was also a Bretwalda, or Britain Ruler, and was the most powerful man in Britain. We know from Bede that Rædwald was Pagan until he was baptized around the year 604, not long after missionaries from the Pope arrived in Kent. Though the Sutton Hoo Treasure had both Christian and Pagan elements, it is clear to me that King Rædwald had a Pagan funeral. I believe he was cremated and his possessions were buried in the earth like his Pagan ancestors; this would account for the lack of human remains at the site and the treasures found within the grave.

Wolves were once numerous in Britain during the Early Middle Ages. Skeletal remains show that they could grow as large as modern Arctic wolves. They were especially numerous in the less-populated areas of Wales and Northumbria. However, an animal which was such a threat to livestock, to human life and which frequently dug up and ate human remains, couldn't be tolerated by the increasing human population, and so the wolf was gradually exterminated by a combination of habitat loss and bounty-hunting. The English wolf was very rare by the late 15th Century, but did survive in the Scottish wilderness until the 17th Century.

In Scottish folklore, on the Shetland Islands, off the coast of Scotland, there was once a werewolf-like creature called the Wulver. The Wulver lived alone and kept to itself. Unlike the traditional werewolf, it was not aggressive if left in peace and couldn't shape-shift. It was believed to be a spirit of some-kind and had never been human.

'The Wulver was a creature like a man with a wolf's head.
He had short brown hair all over him.
His home was a cave dug out of the side of a steep knowe,
half-way up a hill.
He didn't molest folk if folk didn't molest him.
He was fond of fishing, and had a small rock in the deep water,
which is known to this day as the "Wulver's Stane".
There he would sit fishing sillaks and piltaks for hour after hour.
He was reported to have frequently left a few fish on the window-sill of
some poor body.'

Shetland Traditional Lore,
Folklorist, Jessie Margaret Saxby, 1842-1940

The Ghosts of Sutton Hoo

The Sutton Hoo Treasure was found in 1939, Suffolk, East Anglia, on the land owned by Mrs Edith Pretty. After the death of her husband, Col. Frank Pretty, Edith became interested in spiritualism and often travelled to London to consult with a spiritualist medium. One night, Edith told her friend, Dorothy Cox, that she had seen ghosts by the mounds, taking part in a funeral procession. After hearing Edith's story, Dorothy encouraged Edith to have the mounds excavated. In the Spring of 1939, on the eve of World War Two, archaeologist Basil Brown excavated the area and found the famous ghost ship of Sutton Hoo and some of the most beautiful and intricate treasures ever found, crafted and forged by English hands. The ship had long-since rotted away, but it had left a ghostly imprint in the soil, measuring eighty-nine-feet long and fourteen-feet across, and may have been used to carry the Anglo-Saxons to Britain from their Germanic homelands.

Wights

The word 'Wight' from the Old English 'Wiht' is used to describe a supernatural being or nature spirit. Its original meaning may have referred to a small person or dwarf. The modern German and Dutch word 'wicht' is a word used to describe a short person or girl. None of the above words are related to the words witch or wicca. The Wicht, Wichtel or Wichtelchen of Germanic folklore is most commonly translated into English as 'Imp', a small, shy character who often does helpful domestic chores in the home when nobody is looking, as in the Tale of the Cobbler's Shoes.

The Isle of Wight may mean Small Island, or Island of Wights, or it could have been named after a person. Anglo-Saxon names with wight, wiht or similar include Wihtlæg (Offa of Angeln's grandfather), and Wihtgils (Hengist and Horsa's father), or Witta (Hengist and Horsa's grandfather).

To have Land Wights in your area is considered lucky. If you are respectful to the Wights, they will protect the land and continue to make it fertile. At Yule, it was customary to leave fruit and nuts for them under decorated forest trees. This custom manifested into leaving Christmas presents under the Christmas Tree. In Norse Mythology, the Land Wights were known as the Landvættir. An ancient law in Iceland forbade ships from having a dragon-headed prow with a gaping mouth or yawning snout when harbouring, in case it frightened the Landvættir away.

Trolls

Forget the all-singing, all-dancing trolls depicted in modern children's films. Trolls didn't have magical powers, have long pink hair, taste like candy or poop cupcakes. Trolls were fearsome man-eating creatures from what is now Denmark and Scandinavia. They are a type of fairy and were sometimes referred to in Anglo-Saxon literature as ettins or eotenas. In literature, they are described as very tall, at least twice that of a man, and were said to be ugly, hairy, brutish beasts, with tusks and large oversized ears and noses. They are sometimes described as having multiple heads to one body and dwelt in hills, caves or mounds.

The disappearance of people when walking through the forests were often blamed on trolls. People believed they were taken as slaves, or even as pets; and the unlucky ones were eaten raw. Sometimes, the trolls would steal a newborn baby, leaving their own offspring in return, known as a changeling. If your child was born deformed or had learning difficulties, it was surely a troll, switched with your own perfect child, who was now out there, somewhere, living with the troll-folk.

The Scandinavians believed trolls were descended from a Jötunn or Jötnar, meaning 'Mountain-Mover', a hideous race of giants with supernatural strength, who often fought against the Gods. The Jötunns gave their name to Jutland, Northern Denmark. Jutland translates as the 'Land of Trolls'. The first Anglo-Saxon Kingdom in Britain was founded by Hengist and Horsa who came from Jutland.

Trolls were believed to be the cause of bad luck. The Norse believed Thor, God of thunder, used his hammer, Mjölnir (Crusher), to kill them. Wearing a talisman of Thor's hammer around your neck was considered a form of protection against them. Natural stones with man-like features, such as faces or arms and legs, were believed to be trolls petrified by the Sun's bright light. Hence the belief that any troll who hadn't returned to its hiding place by Sunrise would turn to stone.

What were known as trolls in southern Sweden and Denmark were known as huldrefolk in Norway, and vitterfolk in Northern Sweden. The unlucky souls were known as bergtagna, meaning 'those taken to the mountain', which is also the Scandinavian word for 'having been spirited away'. To be bergtagen didn't only refer to the disappearance of a person, but also that upon their return, he or she had been struck with insanity caused by the trolls.

The most famous of all trolls was, of course, Grendel, the grinder of bones, from the Anglo-Saxon poem, Bēowulf, composed between the 7th and 10th Century A. D. Interestingly, the first person to translate the poem into modern English was the Anglo-Saxon professor, J. R. R. Tolkien, author of Lord of the Rings. The poem tells the story of the Gēat warrior, Bēowulf, who travels to Denmark to save the Danes from Grendel, who had been terrorizing King Hrōthgār's hall for the last fifteen years, glutting himself on the flesh of men.

> 'Suddenly the God-cursed brute was creating havoc:
> greedy and grim, he grabbed thirty men
> from their resting places and rushed to his lair,
> flushed up and inflamed from the raid,
> blundering back with the butchered corpses.'

Interestingly, Grendel cannot be hurt by mortal weapons and is killed by Bēowulf tearing his arm off, using nothing but brute strength.

> 'Time and again, Bēowulf's warriors defended their lord's life,
> laying about them as best they could with their ancestral blades.
> Stalwart in action, they kept striking out on every side,
> seeking to cut straight to the soul.
> When they joined the struggle there was something
> they could not have known at the time,
> that no blade on Earth, no blacksmith's art
> could ever damage their demon opponent.'

> 'The monster's whole body was in pain,
> a tremendous wound appeared on his shoulders.
> Sinews split and the bone-lappings burst.
> Bēowulf was granted a glorious victory.'

Grendel's appearance is never described in the poem; it is said he has talons and claws and flaming eyes, but no other description is given and is left to the reader's or listener's imagination.

Sprites

The term 'Sprite' is of Latin origin and comes from 'spiritus'. From this we get the modern word 'spirit', meaning ghost. The Sprites were ghost-like creatures of folklore that lived in the world of the living and the fairy world, the realm of the dead. The modern terms 'sprightly' and 'spirited' comes from the word 'sprite'.

Knuckers

The word 'Knucker' comes from the Old English 'Nicor', which were shape-shifting, mermaid-like water spirits found in Anglo-Saxon, Scandinavian and German folklore. They may get their name from the root word for naked. Grendel's mother in the Bēowulf poem was a Knucker.

In Scandinavian folklore, the Näcken, Näkki and Nøkk were male water spirits who played enchanted songs on the violin, luring women and children to drown in lakes or streams. The enthralling music of the Nøkk was most dangerous to pregnant women and unbaptised children. They were most active during Midsummer's Night, on Christmas Eve and on Thursdays. If the Nøkker attempted to carry someone off, they could be defeated by calling their name, which would be the death of them. It was believed, if you brought the Nøkk three drops of blood, a black animal, or alcohol, he would teach you his enchanting form of music. Though Knuckers are portrayed as malicious in some stories, they are referred to as friendly in others. In Scandinavia, water lilies are called Nix Roses.

In Germany, the German Nix, Nixe and Nixie were river mermen and mermaids who lured men to drown, similar to the Greek Siren and the Scandinavian Näcken. The males could change shape and appear like fish and snakes or even humans, though the females would always retain their fish tails. Descendants of German immigrants to Pennsylvania, in the United States, may refer to a mischievous child as a nixie. The Water Nixie is a German fairy tale collected by William and Jacob Grimm about a Nixie who lived down a well and forced two young children to be her slaves. It can be found amongst the same collection as Rapunzel, Hansel and Gretel, Little Red Riding Hood, and Snow White.

Other mermaid-like water spirits found across England include Jenny Greenteeth, a water hag from Lancashire, who would pull children or the elderly into rivers and drown them. She is described as green-skinned, with long hair and sharp teeth. The name is also used to describe pondweed.

Other Knuckers include the Shellycoat from Scotland, who haunt the River Hermitage and cry out as if drowning, but then laugh at the distracted victim. Peg Powler is a water spirit who lives in the River Tees and drags children into the water if they get too close to the edge. She has green hair and an insatiable hunger for human flesh. The foam or froth which is seen floating on certain parts of the Tees is called 'Peg Powler's suds' or 'Peg Powler's cream'. In Yorkshire and Lancashire, there is the Grindylow, who haunts meres, bogs and lakes and grabs children with their long arms and drowns them.

Serpents

The English have a long and fascinating history with the ocean, from the days when Britannia ruled the waves, going back to the early days of exploration, when English pioneers first began to navigate the globe, right back to the first Anglo-Saxon sea rovers. With all those who frequently ride upon the ocean waves, sailors came home with fascinating stories of the things they saw out there, upon the Deep Blue.

>'The universal dress is the short cloak,
> fastened with a brooch or thorn.
> The richest are distinguished not by loose and flowing clothing,
> but tight and showing the shape of every limb.
> They also wear the pelts of wild animals,
> making careful choice of animal,
> then strip off the pelt and fleck it with patches
> from the skins of beasts that live in the outer ocean and unknown seas.'
>
> Germania,
> Cornelius Tacitus, 9 A. D.

Before his fight with the troll, Bēowulf recounts a battle he had at sea against nine sea-brutes:

>'Each of us swam holding a sword,
> a naked, hard-proofed blade for protection against the whale-beasts.
> The deep boiled up and its wallowing sent the sea-brutes wild.
> Time and again, foul things attacked me, lurking and stalking,
> but I lashed out, gave as good as I got with my sword.
> My flesh was not for feasting on,
> there would be no monsters gnawing and gloating over the banquet
> at the bottom of the sea.
> Instead, in the morning, mangled and sleeping the sleep of the sword,
> they slopped and floated like the ocean's leavings.
> From now on, sailors would be safe,
> the deep sea raids were over for good.
> However it occurred, my sword had killed nine sea-monsters.'

After his victory against the man-eating troll, Bēowulf is given new lodgings. Meanwhile, Grendel's mother sneaks into the hall where the men are asleep and takes her son's claw that Bēowulf had torn from her son. The author of Bēowulf says she is there for revenge, but could he have misunderstood the original story and misunderstood Grendel's mother? To me, it seems she is only there to take her son's remains. She doesn't hurt anyone, not until the warriors wake up and rush for their swords.

>'The hell-dame was in panic, desperate to get out,
> in mortal terror the moment she was found.
> She had pounced and taken one of the retainers
> in a tight hold, then headed for the fen.'

Like I mentioned earlier, it is possible Grendel's mother was a benevolent water spirit; perhaps a Goddess, who simply wanted her son's remains, until she was discovered and forced to defend herself.

> 'Grendles mōdor, ides āglǣc-wīf yrmþe gemunde.'

Grendel's mother is described in the poem as an Ides, which may refer to Valkyries or Goddesses, or perhaps some other form of supernatural female, such as the mermaid-like Knuckers. On a personal note, I don't believe Grendel's mother was a monster at all. I believe she was originally a Knucker or some kind of water spirit, and history has done her a great injustice.

After Hrōthgār's man was taken, Bēowulf and his company track Grendel's mother to a lake infested with serpents.

> 'The water was infested with all kinds of reptiles.
> There were writhing sea-dragons (sǣ-dracan)
> and monsters slouching on slopes by the cliff,
> serpents and wild things such as those that often surface at dawn
> to roam the sail-road and doom the voyage.'

After swimming down to her watery lair, Bēowulf does battle with Grendel's mother and is attacked by droves of sea-beasts who attack him with tusks. Instead of leaving Bēowulf to drown, Grendel's mother drags him to her lair, where a fire is burning brightly. Again, Bēowulf attacks her and she is forced to fight back. Bēowulf cuts her, but her blood is so corrosive that it melts Bēowulf's sword. Then Bēowulf saw amongst her treasure a certain sword, one big enough to have been wielded by a giant.

> 'So the Shieldings' hero, hard-pressed and enraged,
> took a firm hold of the hilt and swung the blade in an arc,
> a resolute blow that bit deep into her neck-bone
> and severed it entirely, toppling the doomed house of her flesh;
> she fell to the floor.'

Later, Bēowulf arrives in Gēatland and informs his kinsman, King Hygelac, of his deeds in Denmark. When describing his battle with Grendel, Bēowulf tells King Hygelac that Grendel carried a pouch intricately strung and fitted with dragon skins that he had used to carry people away with, similar to the sack that Krampus carries to cart away naughty children. Fifty years pass, when a runaway slave finds his way inside an ancient barrow filled with great treasure, but is guarded by a fire-breathing dragon. After the slave takes a cup from the hoard, the dragon awakes and attacks a nearby village.

'Then did the visitant spit forth embers and burn up the bright dwellings;
the flaming ray wrought mischief to men,
for the enemy flying through the air
would leave nothing alive.
He encompassed the people of the land with burning,
with fire and flame.'

It is easy to see where J. R. R. Tolkien got his inspiration from when writing The Hobbit.
Bēowulf, now an old man, is forced to defend the people one last time.

'Inspired again by the thought of glory,
the war-King threw his entire strength behind a sword-stroke
and connected with the skull.'

'Then the bane of that people, the fire-breathing dragon,
was mad to attack for a third time.
When a chance came, he caught the hero in a rush of flame
and clamped sharp fangs into his neck.
Bēowulf's body ran wet with his life-blood;
it came welling out.'

'Once again, the King gathered his strength
and drew a stabbing knife he carried on his belt,
sharpened for battle.
He stuck it deep into the dragon's flank.
Bēowulf dealt it a deadly wound.'

'Then the wound dealt by the ground-burner earlier
began to scald and swell;
Bēowulf discovered deadly poison flowing inside him.'

Though mortally wounded and poisoned, Bēowulf and his kinsman, Wiglaf, manage to slay the dragon, before Bēowulf dies of his injuries, leaving the Kingdom to Wiglaf. The writer(s) of Bēowulf use the words 'draca' and 'wyrm' to describe the dragon. Interestingly, Bēowulf dies much like Thor from Norse Mythology.
   In the Icelandic Saga, known as the Hrólf Kraki Saga, there is a dragon-like creature that is said to be a monstrous beast:

'The creature has wings on its back and it usually flies.
For two autumns now it has come here, causing much damage.
No weapon can bite into it.'

The legendary Siegfried of Xanten, as written in the 12th Century German epic, the Nibelungenlied, is the slayer of a fearsome dragon; though the battle nor the serpent are described in the poem. The Nibelungenlied (Song of the Nibelungs) was inspired by true events, though it was highly fictionalised and resembles more of a Greek tragedy than a work of fantasy. Later poets used the Nibelungenlied as inspiration for the Norse Völsung Saga, featuring Sigurd the Dragon Slayer, which is a mythological version of the Nibelungenlied, complete with Gods, magical spells and talking dragons. Siegfried's tale was also known to the Anglo-Saxons and is mentioned in the Bēowulf poem:

'After his death, Sigemund's (Siegfried's) glory grew and grew
because of his courage when he killed the dragon,
the guardian of the hoard.
Under grey stone he had dared to enter,
all by himself to face the worst.
But it came to pass that his sword plunged
right through those radiant scales
and drove into the wall. The dragon died of it.
His daring had given him total possession of the treasure hoard,
his to dispose of however he liked.
He loaded a boat and weighted her hold with dazzling spoils.
The hot dragon melted.'

It is believed by many that the Normans replaced the story of Siegfried the Dragon Slayer with the story of George and the Dragon. To this day, the flag of England is Saint George's Cross, the fabled Christian dragon slayer, yet the English people have a much older national symbol, the White Dragon. In ancient Welsh legend, as written by Welsh monk, Nennius, in the Historia Brittonum, 828, a white dragon, representing the Anglo-Saxons, does battle with a red dragon, representing the Welsh. The Welsh dragon defeats the white dragon and is symbolic of the Welsh people overcoming the Anglo-Saxon incursions, which is something they never achieved. To this day, the flag of Wales is a red dragon on a green background.

Both Henry of Huntingdon and Matthew of Westminster spoke of a golden dragon being raised at the Battle of Burford in 752 by the West Saxons. The Bayeux Tapestry in France, representing the Norman Conquest of England, depicts a dragon twice, both in the death scene of King Harold. One is a red dragon with white wings held on top of a staff. The other is a fallen dragon, which may represent the fall of Wessex, which makes sense as King Harold was once the Earl of Wessex.

A dragon standard was carried by Henry III in 1216 and was installed at Westminster Abbey. The dragon was also used by Edward III at the Battle of Crécy, 1346, and by Henry V at the Battle of Agincourt, 1415.

Serpents can be found on many surviving Anglo-Saxon treasures, such as the military armour found at the Sutton Hoo burial site in East Anglia. Amongst other fascinating treasures is the golden belt buckle, complete with interlaced, elongated serpents. But none are more impressive than the world famous Sutton Hoo Helmet. At the front of the imposing mask are two elongated serpents facing each other, both with heads, and eyes made of red jewels. One of the dragons forms the crest that runs along the top of the helmet and down the face in a straight line, where it meets a second dragon. The second dragon has a body and tail that make up the mask's nose and moustache. The dragon also has two long wings that give the impression of eyebrows, both ending with a boar's head and lined with red garnets. The entire helmet, including the cheek-pieces, were decorated with warriors in combat and beautiful interlaced-serpents.

In February 2003, during his enthronement at Canterbury Cathedral, Archbishop Rowan Williams wore hand-woven gold silk robes bearing a gold and silver clasp that showed the White Dragon of England and the Red Dragon of Wales.

Today, it is widely accepted that the idea of dragons came to the Anglo-Saxons from China, via the Romans, but I disagree. The word 'dragon' may have, but not the concept. To this day, the rivers in Europe are home to some of the largest species of catfish in the world, fish large enough to swallow a man whole. Long before the advent of science, these giant catfish, growing up to thirteen-feet-long, would have been terrifying to anyone who came across them, with their long, gleaming bodies, large whiskers, humongous mouths and dark eyes. For centuries, there were reports of man-eating serpents in the deep, dark rivers of Europe, and for centuries they were often dismissed as myth and folklore. We now know them as Wels Catfish.

Another giant found in European waters and around the world is the legendary Oarfish, also known as the King of Herring. Washed ashore on a Bermuda beach in 1860, the first known Oarfish was sixteen-feet-long and was thought to be a real-life sea serpent. Though extremely rare to find, the largest on record measured at thirty-six-feet-long. With a long, red dorsal fin, these giants would have been terrifying when spotted by Anglo-Saxon seamen, when the world was still a mystery and the World Serpent still embraced the world of men with its ever tightening coils, threatening to devour any brave soul who dared enter the ocean. Serpents were very real to the Anglo-Saxons, just as Oarfish, Wels Catfish and man-eating sharks are to us today.

Today, many Englishmen and women acknowledge the white dragon as an ethnic symbol of the English people.

Orcs

Orcs are best known from The Lord of the Rings by J. R. R. Tolkien, but Tolkien didn't invent them. The term 'Orc' is Old English, meaning foreigner, monster, or demon, and almost certainly comes from the Latin 'Orcus', the God of the underworld, the equivalent to Hades. The word 'Orc' seems to be related to the Old Dutch 'nork', meaning 'a petulant, crabbed, evil person'.

Though Tolkien didn't invent the term Orc, he is responsible for changing its definition, which now refers to hideous pig and dog-like humanoids, with dark skin, tusks, bad teeth and a taste for human flesh, who ride on the back of wild boars and wargs. In a private letter, Tolkien described the Orcs in his works as 'squat, broad, flat-nosed, sallow-skinned, with wide mouths and slant eyes'. Tolkien must have come across the term 'orcneas' when translating the Bēowulf manuscript:

'þanon untydras ealle onwocon
eotenas ond ylfe ond orcneas
swylce gigantas þa wið gode wunnon
lange þrage he him ðæs lean forgeald.'

'Thence all evil broods were born,
ettins (trolls), elves and orcs,
the giants also, who long time fought with God,
for which he gave them their reward.'

Dwarves

Dwarves are best known in J. R. R. Tolkien's Lord of the Rings, yet dwarves weren't always ginger-haired, wise-cracking, jolly little men who carried large battle-axes. They were once feared creatures with magical abilities, with strong associations with charms, curses, deceit, age and wisdom, but also death and disease. Dwarves are best thought of as the equivalent of Irish Leprechauns.

Dwarves are described as hideous, old in appearance, with long beards, short legs, short-armed, with pale skins, like that of a corpse, and dark hair all over their bodies. The earliest references to dwarves are found in Scandinavia, with references to dwarves being harmed by sunlight, like vampires. They are said to be masters at mining and metal-work. The Dwarves' Cavern in Hasel, Germany, was believed to once house many dwarves. This legend has since given the cavern its name. According to local tradition, on the north and south sides of the Harz mountains, and in areas of the Hohenstein region, there once lived many thousands of dwarves. In the clefts of the cliffs, the dwarf caves still exist.

The Simonside Dwarves were a race of ugly dwarves associated with the Simonside Hills in Northumberland, England. They are also known as Brownmen, Bogles and Duergar. Their leader was said to be called Roarie. After dark, the dwarves led travellers astray, often carrying flaming torches to lead them into bogs. The word 'duergar' is believed to derive from the Old Norse 'dvergar', meaning 'dwarf' or possibly from the northern dialect words for dwarf on the Anglo-Scottish border, such as dorch, dwerch, duerch, duergh and duerwe, all of which come from the Old English 'dweorh' or 'dweorg'.

An Anglo-Saxon Charm Against a Dwarf

'Take seven little wafers, such as those used in worship,
and write these names on each wafer:
Maximianus, Malchus, Iohannes, Martimianus,
Dionisius, Constantinus, Serafion.
Then sing the charm that is given.
First, in the left ear, then in the right ear, then over the top of the head.
And then let a virgin go to him and hang it on his neck.
And do this for three days. He will soon be better.
A spider-thing came on the scene with his cloak in his hand;
claiming you for his horse; he put his cord on your neck.
Then they began to cast off from land; as soon as they left the land
they nonetheless began to cool.
The beast's sister came on the scene; she stopped it,
and swore these oaths: that this should never hurt the sick one,
nor any who tried to take this charm,
nor any who should speak this charm.'

Elves

The word 'elf' comes from the Old English 'ælf' and 'ylfe'. An elf is a creature of Germanic mythology, originally thought to be a race of fertility Gods, who were often viewed as youthful, human-sized men and women of great beauty, living in forests and in underground places or caves, or in wells and springs. Interestingly, the Old English 'ælfsciene', means 'elf-shine' or 'elf-beautiful', proving that elves were once considered beautiful themselves. Also, the word 'oaf' comes from the word 'elf'. An oaf is a person considered to be stupefied by elfish enchantment. The male Anglo-Saxon names, Ælfred, Ælfnoð, Ælfric, Ælfwine, Ælfgar, and the female, Ælfflæd, Ælfwynn and Ælfþryþ, as well as many others, are all named after elves. Elves have been portrayed to be long-lived or immortal, with magical powers that can be used for protection and healing, and could also cross-breed with humans.

In Scandinavia, at the beginning of Winter, the lady of the household would make a blood sacrifice to the elves, called a Álfablót or Elven Sacrifice. It was a time when the crops had been harvested and the animals were fat and awaiting the Winter slaughter. It is likely that the sacrifices were connected to ancestors and fertility, a way to ensure the family was protected during the dark days of Winter, when the dead are able to cross the threshold and torment the living. The Álfablót coincides with the Irish Samhain.

> 'There is a hill, not far from here,
> where elves have their haunt.
> Now get the bull that Kormák killed,
> and redden the outer side of the hill with its blood,
> and make a feast for the elves with its flesh.
> Then you will be healed.'
>
> Kormáks Saga, 10th Century

Over time, perhaps through Christian writers, elves became known as malevolent and something to fear. Elves, like fairies, began to be described as mischievous pranksters that could cause disease to cattle and people, and bring bad dreams to sleepers, known as elf-dreams, where an elf would sit upon your chest throughout the night, giving you nightmares. By the time Bēowulf was written, elves were considered evil:

> 'Thence all evil broods were born,
> ettins (trolls), elves and orcs,
> the giants also, who long time fought with God,
> for which he gave them their reward.'

In order to protect themselves against malevolent elves, Scandinavians could use an elf-cross, which was carved into buildings and woodwork. The elf-cross was a pentagram and was still used in the early 20th Century in Sweden and painted or carved onto doors, walls and household utensils. Another form of elf-cross was an ordinary cross carved onto a round or oblong silver plate, or worn as a pendant on a necklace. The elf-cross wasn't associated with Christianity, though it is likely that Pagans accepted the cross of the Christians because they were already using it as an ancient Pagan symbol. The Anglo-Saxons had a charm against elves, known as Wið færstice:

'If it was the shot of devils, or it was the shot of elves or it was the shot of a witch, now I will help you. This help to you for the shot of devils, this help to you for the shot of elves, this help to you for the shot of a witch; I will help you.'

According to Norse folklore, elves could be seen dancing over meadows at night and on misty mornings. They might leave a circle where they had danced, made of mushrooms, which were called elf circles, or fairy rings; to urinate in one was thought to cause diseases. The Norse believed if a human watched the dance of the elves that a great deal of time would pass in the real world, though it would seem to the viewer that only a short time had passed. Today, elves are associated with Christmas and help Santa make toys for well-behaved children, and are once again remembered in a positive light.

Goblins

A Goblin is a fairy or spirit found across Europe, including England. They are small and grotesque, mischievous or evil, and are greedy for gold and jewellery. They are also believed to have magical abilities. The Redcap is a type of murderous Goblin found along the English-Scottish border. People believed that the border castles were built by the Picts who bathed the foundation stones in human blood which resulted in hauntings. It is believed by some that the Redcaps are the spirits of the original foundation sacrifices.

The Redcap is described as a short, scrumpy old man with long prominent teeth, skinny fingers armed with talons, large fiery red eyes, grisly hair streaming down his shoulders, iron boots, a pikestaff in his left hand, and a red cap on his head. He is also known as Redcomb or Bloody Cap. If a traveller takes refuge in his lair, the Redcap will fling stones at him, and if he manages to kill the intruder, he will soak his cap in their blood. Christians believe the Redcap can only be defeated by repeating Scripture or holding up the Christian cross. The Redcap will then scream and vanish into flames, leaving behind a large tooth on the spot where he was last seen.

In Perthshire, Scotland, the Redcap is depicted as a benign little man living in a room high up in Grantully Castle and bestows good fortune on those who see or hear him. Interestingly, Goblins were said to have originated in Britain and, after boarding ships, later colonised France and the rest of Europe.

Gremlins

Gremlins are a type of fairy that specialises in causing havoc with mechanical devices, such as aircraft. The name 'Gremlin' originated with members of the British Royal Air Force (R.A.F.). In the 1920s, British pilots stationed in Malta, the Middle East and India, claimed Gremlins were responsible for sabotaging aircraft. Gremlins became more widely known during World War Two. The Oxford English Dictionary identifies them as 'the goblins which came out of Fremlin beer bottles'. The word Gremlin may come from the Old English 'gremian', meaning 'to vex.' An early reference to Gremlins is in aviator Pauline Gower's 1938 novel, The ATA: Women with Wings, where she describes Scotland as 'gremlin country', a mystical and rugged territory where scissor-wielding Gremlins cut the wires of biplanes when unsuspecting pilots were about. Spitfire pilots who fought in the Battle of Britain talked of Gremlins in 1940. An article by Hubert Griffith in the Royal Air Force Journal, 18th April 1942, also mentions Gremlins.

Many servicemen swore they saw small creatures tinkering with their equipment. One crewman said he saw a Gremlin before an engine malfunction that caused his B-25 Mitchell Bomber to rapidly lose altitude, forcing the aircraft to return to base. Folklorist, John W Hazen, claimed he found 'a parted cable which bore obvious tooth marks in spite of the fact that the break occurred in a most inaccessible part of the plane.' Hazen also claimed to have heard a musical twang when another cable was parted. It was believed by some that Germany had sent Gremlins to sabotage the R.A.F's war effort.

Bogle

A Bogle is a Northumbrian and Scottish term for a ghost or a type of fairy, and is also an old name for a scarecrow. In fact, Bogles are often depicted like scarecrows, but far more terrifying and were free to move around. The name 'Bogle' comes from the Middle English 'Bugge', which gives us the term 'Bogey Man' or 'Boogie Man'. Today, when we wish to frighten small children, we say the word 'boo'; this comes from the first part of the Bogle's name.

It is said that Bogles never cause harm to mankind, but can cause fear and confusion, such as the case in Northern Ireland, in the 19th Century. On the 31st March, 1866, in County Antrim, Northern Ireland, The Larne Weekly Reporter had an article entitled, 'Bogles in Ballygowan', detailing strange goings on in a rural area. A certain house was attacked at night by stones being thrown through windows, and on one occasion through the roof. The local population were terrified. The disturbances stopped after several months and were blamed on the fact that the house in question had been refurbished using materials from an older house that was apparently the home of the 'little people'.

In Scotland, the Bogle is known as 'Tatty Bogle', who would hide himself in potato fields and either attack unwary humans or cause blight in the patch. The term 'Tatty' is Scottish dialect for 'potato.'

'There's a bogle by the bour-tree at the lang loan heid,
I canna thole the thocht o' him, he fills ma he'rt wi' dreid;
he skirls like a hoolet, an' he rattles a' his banes,
an' gi'es himsel' an unco fash to fricht wee weans.'

The Bogle by the Boor Tree,
W. D. Cocker, 1882-1970

Boggart

The Boggart is a grotesque household spirit or fairy from the North of England. It could also live outside, typically around farms. Like most fairies, it could be benign, but it also had the ability to be cruel and could eat people. Its appearance was quite varied and has been described as relatively human-like in form, though usually uncouth, ugly and often with bestial features. One was described as 'a squat hairy man, strong as a six year old horse, and with arms almost as long as tacklepoles'. The Boggart of Longar Hede from Yorkshire was said to be a fearsome creature the size of a calf, with long shaggy hair and eyes like saucers. It trailed a long chain after itself, which made a noise like the baying of hounds. The Boggart of Hackensall Hall in Lancashire had the appearance of a huge horse. Other Boggarts could take the form of various animals, or even more fearful creatures. The Boggarts of Lancashire had a leader called Owd Hob, who was described with horns, cloven hooves and a tail.

Boggarts who lived in people's homes could be mischievous and make things disappear, cause milk to sour and dogs to go lame. The Boggarts who lived outdoors, in marshes or holes in the ground, were blamed for much darker deeds, such as the abduction of children. In certain areas, such as Northumberland, it was believed that helpful household sprites or fairies, such as Brownies, could turn into malevolent Boggarts if offended or ill-treated.

A Boggart could also be offended if a person attempted to give them a name. A Lancashire Boggart was recorded with the name 'Nut-Nan', who could be heard screaming amongst hazel bushes in Moston, near Manchester. Malevolent Boggarts were known to crawl into people's beds at night and put a clammy hand on their faces. Sometimes, they would pull on the person's ears and strip the bedsheets from them. If the offensive person attempted to move house in order to escape them, the Boggart might follow and continue to haunt them. In England, it is an old Pagan custom to place salt around your house and hang iron horseshoes on your front door or over your fireplace to ward off fairies or bad spirits.

> 'Heavy the beam above the door;
> hang a horseshoe on it
> against ill-luck, lest it should suddenly
> crash and crush your guests.'

Hávamál, 136,

Missing horses and disappearing people were sometimes blamed on Boggarts. The people of Northern England believed Boggarts might have eaten the missing person. In 1861, a report was made about a Boggart in Lancashire, known as The Grizlehurst Boggart. The elderly wife of a farmer reported hearing banging in their farmhouse at night, followed by loud laughter. When the farmer's wife looked outside, she saw three candles casting a blue light and a creature with red burning eyes leaping about. The following morning, the couple found many marks of cloven hooves outside their house. The couple claimed the Boggart had unhitched their horse and overturned their cart on numerous occasions. The couple buried the Boggart at a nearby bend in the road, under an ash tree, with a stake driven through it. Despite being buried, the Boggart was still able to create trouble. The old man was reported saying "Never name it". A Boggart is said to haunt Cave Ha, a limestone cavern at Giggleswick, North Yorkshire. There are many other tales about Boggarts all across Northern England, and there are several places named after them.

Cofgodas

A Cofgod, plural Cofgodas, is Old English for 'Room Gods'. They were believed to be household Gods or spirits, the equivalent to the Ancient Roman Penates. Families in Rome would share a meal together and would toss small bits of food into the fire to feed the household spirits that looked after the family's well-being. The Anglo-Saxon Cofgodas are also very similar to the German Kobolds, a type of fairy spirit that had power over a room. In Germany, it was common practice in the 13th Century to carve effigies of Kobolds and keep them in the house. Sometimes, mandrake roots were used. Though there are stories in Germany of Kobolds turning violent, they were usually peaceful spirits who helped with domestic chores, as long as you were polite and remembered to feed them. If not, then they could play malicious tricks and turn nasty. Interestingly, some legends tell tales of Kobolds wearing red jackets and a cap and being able to fly though the air and enter people's homes through their chimneys.

Fairies

Fairies are a type of Anglo-Saxon Room God or spirit, and come from the Old English 'Færie', which almost certainly has French origins. To modern ears, the word 'demon' conjures up images of devils and bad spirits. Yet the original Greek 'daímōn' simply meant 'good spiritedness' and 'happy', and was used to describe supernatural creatures. The Old English equivalent to 'demon' is 'Færie'. Forget the Victorian-aged, angelic-like creatures of modern myth. Fairies were often described as human-shaped and sized, although they could be tiny, and were very displeasing to the eye. They also had magical powers that could be used for good or evil or mischievous deeds, much like the German Kobolds. The Anglo-Saxons believed they were the spirits of the dead.

Far from their Victorian image, fairies were also known for stealing babies and swapping them for changelings, allowing the human mother to unknowingly breastfeed the fairy baby. Often referred to as 'Celtic folklore', the original people of Great Britain and Ireland once believed in fairies, calling them Pixies or Fays.

As Christianity replaced the native believes of the Anglo-Saxons, fairies were later thought to be a class of demoted angels, and the word 'fairy' was replaced with the Greek word 'demon'. One story involves the angels revolting against God, and so God ordered for the gates of heaven to be closed; those still inside remained angels, those in hell became devils, and those caught in between became fairies. Some believed fairies had been thrown out of heaven, not been good enough, but weren't quite evil enough for hell. As fallen angels, though not quite devils, they could be seen as subjects of the Devil.

Though fairies could be good or bad, they were also known for being mischievous. Waking up in a morning with tangles in your hair were believed to be the work of fairies playing pranks in the night. Have you ever placed an item down, to turn back to it a moment later, only for it to have vanished from sight? That's the work of a fairy, of course. Perhaps you have angered the fairy in some way, maybe by walking too noisily around the house, or screaming during sex. But don't despair, badly behaved fairies can be appeased by leaving out a bowl of porridge at night and by being quiet around the house, especially at night. This custom still survives to this day in England, with the practice of leaving food for Santa and his reindeer on Christmas Eve.

Much of the folklore about fairies revolves around people protecting themselves from their malice. The killing of livestock was often blamed on fairies. If a family member died unexpectedly, the death might be blamed on a fairy kidnapping, swapping the living human with a wooden vessel in the likeness of the missing person. Tuberculosis and other illnesses were sometimes blamed on fairies who forced young men and women to dance every night, causing them to waste away from lack of rest. Fairy trees, such as thorn trees, were dangerous to chop down. One tree was left alone in Scotland and prevented a road been widened for seventy years.

It was an ancient Pagan custom to bring holly into the house to protect the home from fairies. Iron was believed to be poisonous to them. Charms of rowan and herbs were also worn as a form of protection. The crow of cockerels, bread, and four-leaf clovers were used to ward-off fairies, but nothing was more effective in the Christian Middle Ages than the ringing of church bells. In the 16th Century, to believe in fairies was punishable by death.

Imps

Imps are a kind of fairy found in Northern England. Like fairies and other household spirits, they could either be friendly or malevolent. Before the Christianisation of England, it was thought to be good luck to have an Imp living in your home or barn, or under the floorboards. Though described as servants of Satan by Christian writers, the Imps were thought to be mischievous, fun-loving, free-spirited beings, rather than threatening or violent. They are usually described as ugly, yet lively creatures, with tiny statures, and were certainly not considered evil. They were once thought of as attendants to the Gods. If it wasn't for the coming of Christianity, we would still be leaving porridge out for them at night.

Imps were often portrayed as lonely little creatures in search of human attention. They used pranks as a means of attracting human friendship, which often backfired when a person became tired or annoyed by their behaviour, driving it away with certain charms. Even if the Imp was successful in getting the friendship it sought, it would continue to play pranks and jokes, either out of boredom or simply because it was the nature of the Imp. Christians believed Imps were the servants of witches and warlocks and served as spies and informants. During the Christian witch-hunts, leaving food for Imps was considered proof of witchcraft, and the person may have been put to death in the most horrific way.

Hobs and Hobgoblins

Hobgoblins are household fairies or spirits. The term 'Hobgoblin' is actually made up of two words, 'hob' and 'goblin'. In England, the top of a cooker is often referred to as a hob, which is an old word for hearth. They were small, hairy little men and, much like Brownies, dwelt in people's homes and helped with household chores in exchange for gifts of food. Brownies were peaceful creatures, but Hobgoblins were more fond of practical jokes and could be dangerous and easily annoyed.

Brownies

A Brownie is a household spirit or fairy from Scotland and the North of England, similar to the Hob and Hobgoblins. They make their homes in unused parts of the house, such as attics and holes in the walls. Brownies are known as Tomtes and Nisse in Scandinavia. Irish folklorist, Thomas Keightley, 1789-1872, described the Brownie as 'a personage of small stature, wrinkled visage, covered with short curly brown hair, and wearing a brown mantle and hood'. Brownies were believed to live in houses and helped with household chores. Unlike other household spirits, the Brownie doesn't like to be seen and will only work at night, in exchange for small gifts of porridge and honey. It was once customary to leave a seat unoccupied by the fireplace for the Brownie. Interestingly, if a Brownie was mistreated, it was believed it could transform into a malevolent Boggart and become uncontrollable and destructive. In 1703, John Brand wrote about the Brownie:

'Fifty years ago, every family had a Brownie,
or evil spirit, so called, which served them,
to which they gave a sacrifice for his service;
as when they churned their milk, they took a part thereof,
and sprinkled every corner of the house with it, for Brownie's use;
likewise, when they brewed, they had a stone which they called
"Brownie's stane",
wherein there was a little hole into which they poured some wort
for a sacrifice to Brownie.'

Pucks

A Puck was known in Old English as a 'Puca'. A Puck was a small woodland spirit or household fairy. They were mischievous and known to lead travellers astray with echoes and lights in the forest at night, much like Will-o'-the-wisp. Most aches and pains were blamed on spirits of some-kind. Interestingly, the English word 'puking', meaning 'to vomit', may come from the Anglo-Saxon belief that Pucks could cause illness. But if you treated the Puck well, with food and drink, it might do a little housework for you, such as needlework or butter-churning. Like the Imps, Pucks were also known to be lonely creatures and often sought human friendship. Pucks were made famous by William Shakespeare's, A Midsummer Night's Dream, and Rudyard Kipling's, Puck of Pook's Hill, where the Puck refers to himself as 'the oldest Old Thing in England'.

Pucks were also known as Robin Goodfellow or Hobgoblin. The 'Hob' may refer to an 'hearth' and, like the Kobolds, may have been associated with fire. Hobgoblin means 'Fire Goblin'. It is likely that people referred to Hobgoblins as 'Rob' and later 'Robin Goodfellow', because they were afraid to talk about them without raising suspicion from witch hunters. The earliest reference to Robin Goodfellow is found in the Oxford English Dictionary, 1531. To be seen engaging with household spirits was punishable by death, as it was considered witchcraft and Satan Worship.

The Black Shuck

For centuries, the English people have told tales of large black dogs with flaming red eyes that are said to roam the coastlines and countrysides of East Anglia, the Cambridgeshire fens, and Essex. They are also found where the realm of the living and the dead is thin, such as graveyards, cross-roads, bodies of water, dark forests, ancient pathways and places of execution. The dogs vary in size and stature, from large dogs, to the size of a calf or even a horse. Sometimes, they are described as headless, and at other times as floating on a carpet of mist.

In East Anglia, the black dog is known as The Black Shuck. The name 'Shuck' may come from the Old English 'scucca', meaning demon, or possibly from the local dialect word 'shucky', meaning shaggy or hairy.

'He takes the form of a huge black dog,
and prowls along dark lanes and lonesome field footpaths,
where, although his howling makes the hearer's blood run cold,
his footfalls make no sound.
You may know him at once, should you see him,
by his fiery eye; he has but one, and that, like the Cyclops,
is in the middle of his head.
But such an encounter might bring you the worst of luck:
it is even said that to meet him is to be warned that your death
will occur before the end of the year.
So you will do well to shut your eyes if you hear him howling;
shut them even if you are uncertain
whether it is the dog fiend or the voice of the wind you hear.'

Highways & Byways in East Anglia,
W. A. Dutt, 1901

The earliest surviving description of devilish black hounds in England is recorded in the Peterborough Chronicle, 1127:

> 'Let no one be surprised at the truth
> of what we are about to relate,
> for it was general knowledge throughout
> the whole country that immediately after his arrival,
> many men saw and heard a great number of huntsmen hunting.
> The huntsmen were black, huge, and hideous,
> and rode on black horses and on black he-goats,
> and their hounds were jet black, with eyes like saucers, and horrible.'

On the 4th August, 1577, in Blythburgh, Suffolk, East Anglia, as a great storm raged above, the locals gathered inside the church for safety, when the Black Shuck is said to have burst through the doors of Holy Trinity Church to a clap of thunder. The black dog ran up the nave, past a large congregation, killing a man and boy and causing the church steeple to collapse through the roof. As the dog left, it left scorch marks on the north door which can be seen to this day. On the same day, at Saint Mary's Church, Bungay, in Suffolk, a similar attack was described in A Straunge and Terrible Wunder by Abraham Fleming, 1577:

> 'This black dog, or the devil in such a likeness,
> running all along down the body of the church with great swiftness,
> and incredible haste, among the people, in a visible form and shape,
> passed between two persons, as they were kneeling upon their knees,
> and occupied in prayer as it seemed,
> wrung the necks of them both at one instant clene backward,
> in so much that even at a moment where they kneeled,
> they strangely died.'

The scorch marks on the door are referred to by the locals as 'the Devil's fingerprints'. The event is remembered in this verse:

> 'All down the church in midst of fire,
> the hellish monster flew, and,
> passing onward to the quire,
> he many people slew.'

On Dartmoor, Richard Cabell was said to have been a huntsman who sold his soul to the Devil. When he died in 1677, black hounds appeared around his burial chamber. His ghost is said to ride with black dogs. It is believed that this tale inspired Arthur Conan Doyle to write his well-known story, The Hound of the Baskervilles, about a fiendish black ghost dog that haunts Dartmoor.

In Lancashire, the black hound is called a Barghest, meaning borough ghost. A black dog has been said to haunt the Newgate Prison for over four hundred years, appearing before executions. According to legend, in 1596, a scholar was sent to the prison for witchcraft, but was killed and eaten by starving prisoners before he could face trial. The dog was said to appear soon after and, although the terrified men killed their guards and escaped, the beast is said to have haunted them wherever they fled. Black Dog Hill and Black Dog Halt Railway Station in Wiltshire are named after a ghost dog which is said to be found in the area. According to some legends, seeing the dog is an omen of death. In some cases, after seeing the Black Shuck, witnesses have claimed their loved ones soon fell ill or died.

In other accounts, the Black Shuck is regarded as benign and said to accompany women on their way home, in the role of protector. Some black dogs have been said to help lost travellers find their way home and are more often helpful than threatening. The Gurt Dog or Great Dog of Somerset is an example of a benevolent dog. It was said that mothers would allow their children to play unsupervised on the Quantock Hills, because they believed the Gurt Dog would protect them. It would also accompany lone travellers in the area, acting as a protector and guide. In Lincolnshire, there is a ghost dog known locally as Hairy Jack. He is believed to haunt the fields and village lanes around Hemswell, and there has been reported sightings throughout the county, from Brigg to Spalding. Author and folklorist, Ethel Rudkin, claimed to have seen Hairy Jack herself and formed the impression that black dogs in Lincolnshire were mainly of a gentle nature and looked upon as a spiritual protector.

The Church Grim

The Church Grim is a figure from English and Scandinavian folklore, a ghost dog that oversees the welfare of a particular church. Church Grims are said to enjoy loud ringing bells and often appear as black dogs, but can be seen as rams, horses, roosters, ravens, or as small, misshapen, dark-skinned people. It was believed that the first man buried in a new churchyard had to guard it against the Devil. To save a human soul from this duty, it became customary to find a black dog and then bury it alive on the north side of the churchyard, creating a guardian spirit. In Scandinavia, a lamb would sometimes take the place of the dog.

In May 2014, a seven-foot dog was found at the 14th Century Leiston Abbey in Suffolk, in a nameless grave, with pottery fragments covering its body. Carbon-dating of the bones indicated a date of either 1650-1690 or 1730-1810. The dog's skeleton was analysed by a veterinarian who approximated its weigh at around two hundred pounds when it lived. He also concluded that the dog would stand seven-feet-tall if it stood on its hind legs. I believe I am the first person to acknowledge the dog's remains as potentially a Church Grim.

Bloody-Bones and Rawhead

Found across England, there is a bogeyman known as Bloody-Bones or Rawhead. He is described as a naked giant, with pale skin and great, grasping hands. The flesh on his head is described as raw and oozing, his flesh stripped away from his skull, exposing the muscle and veins. He has wide, staring eyes and rivulets of blood running down his face and dripping onto his chest. According to legend, he lurks in lakes and ponds waiting for his prey. Or in his den, piled high with the gnawed bones of children, where he sits and waits; his long arms clasped around his long bony legs, which he keeps tucked under his chin. When he senses prey, he unfolds his limbs like a waking spider.

In Somerset folklore, Bloody-Bones is said to live in the homes of naughty children, hiding in a dark cupboard, usually under the stairs. If you were brave enough to peep through a crack, you would get a glimpse of the crouching creature, with blood running down his hideous face, sitting on a pile of bones that had once belonged to naughty children.

> 'Rawhead and Bloody Bones
> steals naughty children from their homes,
> takes them to his dirty den,
> and they are never seen again.'
>
> An Old English Nursery Rhyme

Night Mære

Today, the term 'nightmare' refers to bad dreams, but in fact the term comes from something much older and much darker. A Mare, from the Old English 'Mære', is an ancient female spirit or elf-like creature found in Germanic folklore and all around the world. They are believed to ride on people's chests while they sleep, creating the sensation of breathlessness and panic, and causing bad dreams or nightmares, similar to the Jewish Succubus (female) and Incubus (male).

The Night Mære is often referred to as 'the Night Hag', and she invokes terrifying dreams to her victims. Sometimes, the sleeping person believed that they had been riding wild, demonic horses all night in their dreams. I believe I am the first person to suggest they may have been forced to join Wōden and the Wild Hunt. The Mære herself was also believed to ride

horses and was often blamed for tangling a sleeping person's hair, called mare-locks, mare-braids, or mare-tangles. Certain trees that were undersized or twisted, with entangled branches, were believed to be ridden by a Mære.
In Germany, they were known as Mara, Mahr or Mare. A Westphalian charm to ward off Mæres, reads:

'Here I am lying down to sleep; no nightmare shall plague me
until they have swum through all the waters that flow upon the earth
and counted all stars that appear in the skies.
Thus help me God Father, Son, and Holy Ghost. Amen!'

Witches

The Old English 'wicca' means 'wise man'. The Old English 'wicce' means 'wise woman'. From these words we get the word witch. The term 'witchcraft' comes from the Old English 'wiccecræft'. The Old English 'hægtesse' means 'witch fury', and gives us the word 'hag'. The Old English 'hellrūna', is another term for a witch. The Old English phrase, 'swa wiccan tæcaþ', means 'as the witches teach'.

Witches and witchcraft have nothing to do with Halloween, Samhain, Devil worship or child sacrifice, and did not have any negative connotations until coming into contact with Christianity. Witches in pre-Christian Anglo-Saxon England, as well as on the continent, were seen as divine and helped to protect holy springs and hallowed groves from troublesome fairies, goblins and unclean spirits. They used magic to protect women during pregnancy and to invoke the spirits of their ancestors and the Goddesses to help bless the new ones amongst the clan. The witches were loved by the people and cast healing spells and used their vast knowledge of plants and herbs to cure sickness and deliver newborns. They were housewives, mothers, daughters, sisters, aunts and grandmothers. They were the keepers of the house, nurses, midwives, teachers and warriors, and a portal to the realm of the Gods.

'Thou shalt not suffer a witch to live.'

The Bible, Exodus 22:18

Christianity has done Pagan women a great disservice. Christians were led to believe the only way to heal a person was through the power of prayer and the Christian church. And the church tolerated no competition. In the year 306, Constantine the Great, 272-337, became the new Emperor of the Roman Empire, and was Rome's first Christian ruler. He decreed that all witches should be killed and have their flesh torn from their bones with iron hooks. In the year 415, a wise woman called Hypatia, in Alexandria (Egypt), was accused of witchcraft. A mob of Christians attacked her, took her to their church, stripped her, and gouged out her flesh using broken tiles, before burning her dead body. Her only crime was to practice mathematics.

The Christian Bible has the oldest known punishments for witchcraft:

> 'A man or woman that has a familiar spirit,
> or is a wizard, shall surely be put to death:
> they shall stone them with stones:
> their blood shall be upon them.'
>
> Leviticus 20:27

The Paenitentiale Halitgari, written in 6th Century Ireland, states:

> 'Some men are so blind that they bring their offering to earth-fast stone
> and also to trees and to wellsprings,
> as the witches teach, and are unwilling to understand
> how stupidly they do or how that dead stone
> or that dumb tree might help them
> or give forth health when they themselves are never
> able to stir from their place.'

The 6th Century Roman historian, Jordanes, wrote about witches in his famous work, The Origin and Deeds of the Goths:

> 'But after a short space of time, the race of the Huns,
> fiercer than ferocity itself, flamed forth against the Goths.
> We learn from old traditions that their origin was as follows:
> Filimer, King of the Goths, son of Gadaric the Great,
> who was the fifth in succession to hold the rule of the Getae
> after their departure from the island of Scandza (Scandinavia),
> - and who entered the land of Scythia with his tribe, -
> found among his people certain witches,
> whom he called in his native tongue Haliurunnae (Hellrūna).
> Suspecting these women, he expelled them from the midst of his race
> and compelled them to wander in solitary exile afar from his army.
> There, the unclean spirits, who beheld them as they wandered through the
> wilderness, bestowed their embraces upon them and begat this savage
> race, which dwelt at first in the swamps,
> –   a stunted, foul and puny tribe, scarcely human,
> –   and having no language save one which bore slight resemblance
> to human speech. Such was the descent of the Huns who came to
> the country of the Goths.'

The Paenitentiale Theodori, written in 7th Century England, is one of the oldest handbooks for Christian priests explaining the type of penance required for indulging in witchcraft:

'If a woman has performed incantations or diabolical divinations, let her do penance for one year. About which it says in the canon: Those who observe auguries or auspices or dreams or any kind of divinations according to the customs of the heathens, or introduce men of this kind into their homes in investigating a device of the magicians - if these repent, if they are of the clergy let them be cast out, but if they are truly secular people, let them do penance for five years.'

The Paenitentiale Ecgberhti, written in 8th Century England, states:

'If a woman acts with wizardry, enchantment and drugs, and succeeds, let her fast 12 months on bread and water.'

In Ireland, Dame Alice Kyteler was accused of witchcraft. She fled the country, but her servant, Petronilla de Meath, was caught and tortured, until confessing to witchcraft. She was burned to death at the stake on 3rd November 1324. The term 'heretic' comes from the Greek 'hairesis' and means 'to choose' or 'to think freely'. In 1326, Pope John XXII authorized the inquisition to prosecute witchcraft as heresy, which gave rise to the infamous witch trials that followed. An estimated sixty thousand innocent women were executed in the most unspeakable ways. In 1431, the Anglo-Normans captured Joan of Arc and burned her alive for witchcraft. She was nineteen-years-old when she died. In 1542, King Henry XIII introduced a law in England that anyone conjuring up evil spirits would be killed and their wealth would go to the Crown. Luckily, the law only lasted for six years and only one man was arrested before being set free. In 1609, the infamous Bamberg Witch Trials begin in what is now Germany. The Christian bishop, Gottfried von Dornheim, became a witch hunter. He received the wealth of his victims and had hundreds of innocent people executed.

Born in England, 1620, Matthew Hopkins was a witch hunter, responsible for the murder of three hundred English women between 1644 and 1646. Although torture was unlawful, Hopkins used techniques such as sleep deprivation to extract confessions from his victims. He would also cut the arm of the accused with a blunt knife; if she didn't bleed, she was said to be a witch. He would also tie women to chairs and throw them into rivers. If they floated, they were 'proven' to be witches and were murdered. If they sank, then they simply drowned. After being warned about the drownings, Hopkins and his assistants began to search their victims for the Devil's mark, such as moles, birthmarks or an extra nipple. If the suspected witch had no visible marks, then he would shave all of their body hair and prick them with needles and knives, expecting the witches' familiar, such as a cat or dog, to drink the blood from the wound as proof they were a witch. According to legend, Hopkins was later accused of unlawful torture and murder and was subjected to his own swimming test and was executed as a witch in 1647.

In 1684, Alice Molland was the last woman to hang in England after being accused of witchcraft. Eight years later, in 1692, the infamous Salem Witch Trials begin in America, ending with the death of nineteen women and an eighty-year-old man who took two days to die, lying under a pile of stones. In 1945, Charles Walton was found near Long Compton, Warwickshire, England, pinned to the ground by a pitchfork. The locals claimed he was a witch. His murderer was never found.

The practice of concealing witch-bottles in one's home, holding personal items, typically from someone suffering an illness and believing themselves persecuted by a witch, began in the 16th Century, as a protection from witches. The majority of the bottles found were small, pot-bellied and had a face of a grim-looking bearded man. In 2004, a witch bottle was discovered by builders in Greenwich, south-east London. The bottle was unopened and had all of its original contents inside. It is believed to be the world's most complete witch bottle. CT scans and chemical analysis, along with gas chromatography, revealed the contents of the bottle, which included human urine, brimstone, twelve iron nails, eight brass pins, human hair, navel fluff, a piece of heart-shaped leather, pierced by a bent nail, and ten fingernail clippings. The use of iron nails suggests that it was used not just for witches, but maybe ghosts or household spirits, such as fairies, because iron was believed to repel them. In England, it is customary to surround Christian churches with an iron fence to contain the souls of the dead. Burying an iron knife under the entrance to one's home was also used to keep witches from entering.

Behind the hearth of an old 17th Century cottage in Broughton, Cambridgeshire, a dried out cat and rat were found placed inside a box. Their bodies had been preserved by the heat of the fire in the chimney. Like the witch bottle at Greenwich, they were put there to protect the house from witches.

By the early 18th Century, the witch hunts had declined, culminating with the British Witchcraft Act of 1735, but there were several witch trials during the second half of the 18th Century; the last known dating to 1833, Tennessee, USA.

The modern image of a witch was first made popular in England during the 17th Century. Surprisingly, it may come from England's female ale brewers. Until the 15th Century, ale brewing was done primarily by women. They were known in England as alewives or brewsters. They wore big black pointy hats in order to stand out from the crowd while selling ale. They also kept cats to keep rats and mice away from their barrels of grain, and used black cauldrons to brew the ale. A broom was used as a sign that beer was available to purchase. Interestingly, the Norse Goddess, Freyja, has a chariot that is pulled along by big black cats. Because of their association with a Pagan Goddess, black cats became associated with witchcraft.

In Medieval Europe, the church feared the vices that came with the consumption of alcohol and began to portray the alewives negatively. In 1540, the English City of Chester ordered that no women between the ages of fourteen and forty would be permitted to sell ale, in the hopes of limiting the trade to only women above or below an age of sexual desirability. The alewives were accused of being disobedient to their husbands, sexually deviant and cheating their customers with watered-down ale and high prices. The alewives were depicted in church murals as someone who belonged in hell. Poems such as John Skelton's, The Tunning of Elynour Rummyng, The Tale of Beryn and Mother Bunch of Pasquil's Jests all depicted alewives as repulsive figures. However, some women did continue to sell ale into the 17th Century until the infamous Witch Trials began.

Conclusion

'Women were near equal companions to the males in their lives,
such as husbands and brothers,
much more than in any other era before modern time.'

Women in Anglo-Saxon England,
Christine Fell, 1984

Anglo-Saxon England was the first place in history where women were raised to sainthood and convents were run by an Abbess, who was responsible for finances and management. Documents of wills and charters show that women were left entire estates by their loved ones, including slaves, livestock, household furnishings, clothes, jewellery and books. The equal status men and women shared in England continued until the Norman Conquest of 1066, at which point women were viewed as unimportant.

During the Victorian Period, English women were arrested and placed inside insane asylums for as little as reading books and studying, being kicked in the head by a horse, suffering anxiety, grief and depression, political excitement, domestic trouble, losing sons through wars, amongst many others. Since 1066, women have been oppressed, demonised, falsely accused of witchcraft, beaten, publicly humiliated, drowned, thrown into mental asylums, raped, tortured and burned at the stake.

Today, we live in an age of decadence and decay, where life is no longer sacred, and healthcare comes at a price; when young ones are murdered in their mother's womb; a time when men and women are encouraged to hate one another; a time of religious and economic conflict; a time when our leaders worship the economy and serve bankers as their Gods; where mankind pollutes his own seas, tears down his forests, poisons the food we eat, the air we breathe, pours fluoride into our water supply; a time when our media teaches us to fear and to hate. We live in a time when our young men and women are taught that they have no value.

I promise you, it was better before, when we were Pagans, and all life was sacred, when every child was thought a blessing from the Gods. There were happier times than this, when the people would come together to worship the Gods, to sing and dance, to cure sickness and disease; a time when men and women fought side by side to protect what they loved; when marriage was holy, and men worshipped their women as Goddesses.

'Their whole life is occupied in hunting
and in the pursuits of the military art;
from childhood they devote themselves to fatigue and hardships.
Those who have remained chaste for the longest time,
receive the greatest praise among their people.
They think a lack of intercourse makes the young men taller,
stronger and more muscular.
To have had knowledge of a woman
before the twentieth year is considered scandalous.
They attempt no concealment the facts of sex;
men and women bathe together in the rivers
and only use skins or small cloaks of deer hides,
a large portion of the body being left naked.'

Julius Caesar,
The Conquest of Gaul, 1st Century A. D.,
writing about the Germanic Pagans

'They also carry into the fray figures
and emblems taken from their sacred groves.
Not chance or the accident of mustering makes the troop or wedge,
but family and friendship,
and this is a very powerful incitement to valour.
A man's dearest possessions are at hand;
he can hear close to him the laments of his women

and the wailing of his children.
These are the witnesses that a man reverences most,
to them he looks for his highest praise.
The men take their wounds to their mothers and wives,
and the women are not afraid of counting and examining the blows,
and bring food and encouragement to the fighting men.'

'For all that, marriage in Germania is strict,
and there is no feature in their morality that deserves higher praise.
They are almost unique among barbarians
in being satisfied with one wife each.
The exceptions, which are exceedingly rare,
are of men who receive offers of many wives because of their rank;
there is no question of sexual passion.
The dowry is brought by husband to wife, not by wife to husband.
Parents and kinsmen attend and approve of the gifts;
gifts not chosen to please a woman's whim or gaily deck a young bride,
but oxen, horse with reins, shield, spear and sword.
For such gifts a man gets his wife,
and she in her turn brings some present of arms to her husband.
In this interchange of gifts they recognize the supreme bond,
the holy mysteries, the presiding deities of marriage.
A woman must not imagine herself free to neglect
the manly virtues or immune from the hazards of war.
That is why she is reminded, in the very ceremonies which bless her
marriage, that she is coming to share a man's toils and dangers,
that she is to be his partner in all his sufferings and adventures,
whether in peace or war. That is the meaning of the team of oxen,
of the horse ready for its rider, of the gift of arms.
On these terms she must live her life and bear her children.
She is receiving something that she must hand over unspoilt and treasured
to her children, for her son's wives to receive in their turn and pass on to
the grandchildren.'

'Thus it is that the German women live in a chastity that is impregnable,
uncorrupted by the temptations of public shows
or the excitements of banquets.
Clandestine love-letters are unknown to men and women alike.
Adultery in that populous nation is rare in the extreme.
Neither beauty, youth nor wealth can find the sinner a husband.
No one in Germania finds vice amusing,
or calls it 'up-to-date' to debauch and be debauched.
It is still better with those states in which only virgins marry,
and the hopes and prayers of a wife are settled once and for all.
They take one husband, like the one body or life that they possess.

No thought or desire must stray beyond him.
To restrict the number of children
or to put to death any born after the heir is considered criminal.
Good morality is more effective in Germania
than good laws in some places that we know.'

'The children grow up in every home, naked and dirty,
to that strength of limb and size of body which excite our admiration.
Every mother feeds her child at the breast
and does not depute the task to maids and nurses.
The master is not to be distinguished from the slave by any pampering in
his upbringing. They grow up together among the same flocks and on the
same ground, until maturity sets apart the free and the spirit of valour
claims them as her own. The young men are slow to mate, and their
powers, therefore, are never exhausted.
The girls, too, are not hurried into marriage.
As old and full-grown as the men,
they match their mates in age and strength,
and the children reproduce the might of their parents.
Childlessness in Germania is not a paying profession.'

'It stands on record that armies wavering on the point of collapse
have been restored by the women.
They have pleaded heroically with their men,
thrusting their bosoms before them and forcing them to realize
the imminent prospect of their enslavement
– a fate which they fear more desperately for their women
– than for themselves.
It is even found that you can secure a surer hold on a state
if you demand among the hostages girls of noble family.
More than this, they believe that there resides in women
an element of holiness and prophecy, and so they do not scorn
to ask their advice or lightly disregard their replies.
In the reign of the deified Vespasian,
we saw Veleda long honoured by many Germani as a divinity,
whilst even earlier they showed a similar reverence for Aurinia and
others; a reverence untouched by flattery or any pretence of turning
women into goddesses.'

Germania,
Cornelius Tacitus, 9 A. D.

Also available by S. A. Swaffington:

Germania
Offa: Rise of the Englisc Warrior
Ket and Wīg: A Song of Vengeance
Siegfried the Dragon Slayer

Printed in Great Britain
by Amazon